THE music kit

fourth edition

THE music kit

fourth edition

Rhythm Reader and Scorebook

Tom Manoff

Computer Programs by

John Miller, North Dakota State University

Peter Hesterman, Eastern Illinois University

with **Tom Manoff**

W. W. NORTON & COMPANY

NEW YORK · LONDON

Manoff, Tom.
The music kit / Tom Manoff ; computer programs by
 John Miller, Peter Hesterman with Tom Manoff.—4th ed.
        p. cm.
Contents: [1] Workbook — [2] Rhythm reader and scorebook.
ISBN 0-393-97402-2 (pbk.)
1. Music theory—Elementary works. I. Title.

MT7 .M267 2001
781.2—dc21
2001030582

The text is composed in Myriad

Composition by Willow Graphics

Manufactured in the United States by LSC Communications

Book design by Joan Greenfield

Cover illustration *Arrangement II* by Gil Mayers
    Private Collection/Gil Mayers/Superstock

ISBN 0-393-97402-2 (Regular Version, pbk.), 0-393-97403-0
    (Computer-Assisted Version, pbk.)

W. W. Norton & Company, Inc., 500 Fifth Avenue, New York,
    N.Y. 10110

www.wwnorton.com

W. W. Norton & Company Ltd., 15 Carlisle Street,
    London W1D 3BS
        5 6 7 8 9 0

Contents

Rhythm Reader

Contents

Melodies

Chorales

From the Classical Tradition

Popular and Jazz Tunes

Rhythm Reader

Chapter One

Rhythm, Beat and Tempo

Rhythm is action in time. Whether the action is the sound of a symphony, the crash of a cymbal, or the ticking of a clock, it has a specific rhythm that occurs in time. **Rhythmic notation** is the system we use to indicate the number of actions in music, the amount of time each action takes, and the relationship of these actions to a basic ongoing pulse, called the **beat**. This beat is what we feel when we step in time to a marching band or tap our feet to a catchy tune. The **tempo**, or speed, of the beat can vary considerably. A polka has a fast tempo; a funeral march, a slow tempo. The rhythms we *hear* are represented by symbols we *see*; these are called **notes**.

Quarter Note and Eighth Note

The first notes we learn are the quarter note (♩ or ♩) and the eighth note (♪ or ♪) Quarter notes are twice as long in duration as eighth notes; conversely, two eighth notes equal the duration of one quarter note.

$$♩ = ♪♪$$

The several parts of the eighth note are the **notehead**, **stem**, and **flag**:

stem → ♪ ← flag
notehead →

Beaming Eighth Notes

Eighth notes can be beamed together for easier reading.

beam
♪♪ = ♫

♪♪♪♪ = ♫♫

beam

1 Rewrite these eighth notes, using beams.

Example

♪ ♪ ♪ = ♫♫♫

a.

♪ ♪ ♪ ♪ =

b.

c.

Speaking Rhythms

In this book we will learn two methods of speaking rhythms. The first, used in Chapters One through Three, consists of saying two easy syllables: "ta" for quarter notes (♩ or ♪) and "tee" for eighth notes (♪, ♪, ♫, or ♫). This method, used in *Rhythms 1–12* (pp. 4–6, 9–10, and 18), has had considerable success with students of all ages—particularly those with no prior knowledge of rhythmic notation—and has proven valuable in various teaching situations.

The second method is introduced in Chapter Two on the very same rhythmic patterns (*Rhythms 1a–12a*) (pp. 14 and 19). This method consists of saying numbers for quarter notes and the word "and" for eighth notes, and will be employed for the remainder of the book. You may begin learning rhythms with either method; both are recorded on the accompanying CD.

2

a. Listen to *Rhythm 1* (CD, track 13) a few times, then speak the rhythm with the recording. Before each exercise, a background rhythm and count establish the tempo. For this example, the count is "one, two, three, four," which appears below in parentheses.

b. Repeat *Rhythm 1*, speaking and following the version below; it is the same rhythm as the one above, but notated differently.

Double Bar   A double bar (‖ or ▌) indicates the end, as in exercise #2, above.

Repeat Signs   A group of notes is repeated when it is enclosed by **repeat signs**, (‖: :‖) For example:

Sometimes the repeat sign appears only at the end of a group of notes or section of a piece. For example:

3 Write out each of these rhythms without using repeat signs.

Example

a.

b.

c.

When performing a line of music that repeats, go back to the beginning without any lapse of the beat when you reach the repeat sign.

4 Speak *Rhythms 1* through *3* with the CD (tracks 13–15). Remember to observe any repeat signs. The counts appear in parentheses.

a. *Rhythm 1*: (1 2 3 4)

b. *Rhythm 2*: (1 2 3 4)

c. *Rhythm 3*: (1 2 3)

5 Repeat *Rhythms 1* through *3* with the CD. This time tap or clap. Don't speak. Follow the notation in exercise 4, above.

6 Repeat *Rhythms 1* through *3* with the CD. The versions below sound the same as in exercise 4, but are notated differently. Speak and clap.

a. *Rhythm 1*: (1 2 3 4)

b. *Rhythm 2*: (1 2 3 4)

c. *Rhythm 3*: (1 2 3)

7 Do these on your own. Speak first, then clap or tap the rhythms.

a.

b.

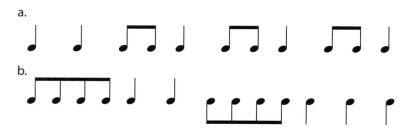

8 Tap these rhythms. Don't speak!

a.

b.

c.

d.

Fermata Sign

The **fermata** symbol (⌢), when placed above or below a note, indicates that the note is to be held for a longer duration than its normal value. The exact duration is left to the discretion of the performer. The fermata is sometimes called a **hold**.

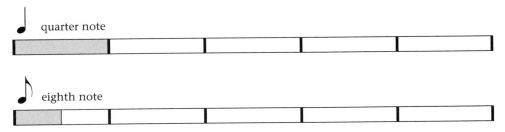

Notes Control Space

The written note controls a space on the page in the same way that the sound it represents controls a period of time. To represent this relationship visually we will use a "Rhythm Spacer," a grid that shows how much space and time different notes take up. We will find that notes of longer duration control more space on the page than those of shorter duration.

The value of each box on the Rhythm Spacer below equals one quarter note. Observe the amount of space that the quarter note and eighth note use, represented by the shaded areas:

Rhythm Spacer

To represent the eighth note on the Rhythm Spacer, it is necessary first to divide the quarter-note box in half with a line, and then to shade one half of the box.

9   Line up the following groups of notes above the Rhythm Spacer. Draw vertical lines under the eighth notes, and then shade each box to represent the correct values of the quarter and eighth notes. Study the example carefully.

Example

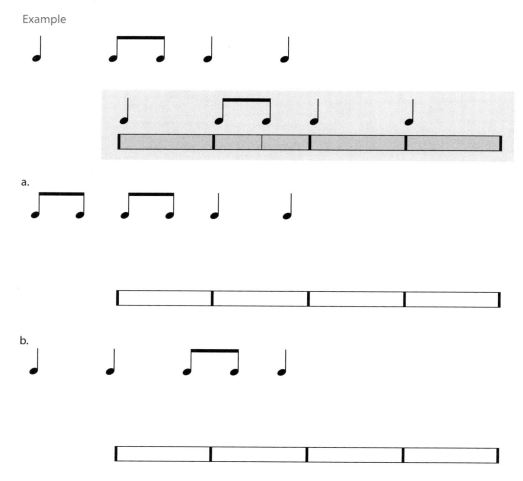

a.

b.

TERMS, SYMBOLS, AND CONCEPTS

rhythm
beat
basic pulse
duration
tempo
♩ quarter note
♪ eighth note
note

notehead
stem
flag
beaming eighth notes

notes control space

Chapter Two

Rests

Just as there are symbols that represent musical sounds, there are symbols that represent the absence of musical sound. These are called **rests**. A **quarter rest** (𝄽) has the same time value as a quarter note. In the following rhythms, speak the quarter rest as "rest."

1

Speak these rhythms with the CD (tracks 16–19). Do not tap.

a. *Rhythm 4*: (1 2 3 4)

Speak: ta ta rest ta ta rest ta ta

b. *Rhythm 5*: (1 2 3 4)

c. *Rhythm 6*: (1 2 3 4)

d. *Rhythm 7*: (1 2 3 4)

2

Repeat *Rhythms 4* through *7*. Speak and tap along with the CD. Do not tap rests; just say "rest," as on the recording.

3

Repeat these new notations of *Rhythms 4* through *7*. Speak and tap along with the CD.

a. *Rhythm 4*: (1 2 3 4)

b. *Rhythm 5*: (1 2 3 4)

c. *Rhythm 6*: (1 2 3 4)

d. *Rhythm 7*: (1 2 3 4)

Rests Control Space

Although the quarter rest represents silence, like the quarter note it controls space on the page. The silence has a duration, and when placed on the Rhythm Spacer, the quarter rest takes up one box. To differentiate between a quarter rest and a quarter note on the Rhythm Spacer, we will lightly shade the space that the rest occupies.

4 Place the following rhythms on the Rhythm Spacer. Draw vertical lines under the eighth notes. Use a lighter shading for the rests than for the notes, as in the diagram above.

a.

b.

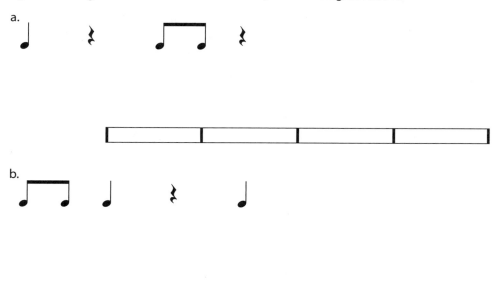

Meter and Bar Lines

We naturally hear rhythm in groups of beats. For example, think how often you hear a "tic" followed by a "toc." In music notation, this grouping of beats is called **meter**. Some common groupings are two, three, and four beats. Each group is called a **measure** and is enclosed between two vertical lines, called **bar lines**.

Rhythms with Meter

Strong and Weak Beats

We can often recognize measure divisions when we hear **strong** or **accented** beats followed by **weak** or **unaccented** beats. The first beat of a measure is the strongest. We call this beat the **downbeat**. In the following exercise, the downbeats are indicated by **accent signs** (>).

5

Speak and tap these rhythms. Accent the downbeats by speaking or tapping them a little louder.

f.
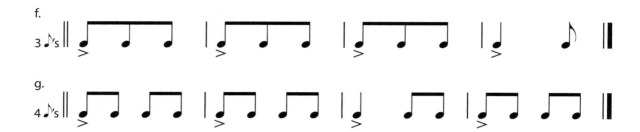

g.

Time Signatures

The meter of a piece is given by a **time signature**, which consists of an upper number indicating how many beats are in each measure, and a lower number indicating which kind of note equals one beat.

| $\frac{4}{4}$ | 4 beats per measure |
| quarter note = 1 beat |

6 In the boxes below, write the meaning of the numbers in the indicated signatures, as illustrated above.

a. $\frac{3}{8}$

b. $\frac{3}{4}$

c. $\frac{4}{4}$

d. $\frac{2}{4}$

e. $\frac{3}{8}$

f. $\frac{4}{8}$

Counting Beats

Speaking the number of each beat in a measure is the most common way of counting. This practice not only provides a steady reference to the basic pulse, it also keeps track of where a note or rhythm is within a measure.

7 Count each pulse with a steady, even beat:

Metronome and Tempo

A **metronome** is a mechanical device that supplies a basic pulse at specific tempos. For example, set a metronome at 60, and you will hear 60 even pulses per minute; set it at 100, and you will hear 100 pulses per minute, and so forth. A metronome marking is specified by the letters M.M. with an indication of what kind of note is represented by the basic pulse; for example, M.M. ♩ = 120. A metronome will come in quite handy as you work through the *Rhythm Reader*.

Division of the Basic Pulse

To count rhythms that include notes shorter than the basic pulse one can use the following system: the quarter note represents the basic pulse, and each beat that is divided into eighth notes is given the syllable "and" on the second eighth note.

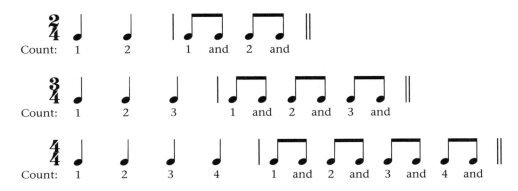

8

Listen to *Rhythms 1a-7a* on the CD (tracks 25–31), observing how the count indicates notes *and* rests. The rhythms are played on various instruments. Do not tap the rhythms. When you are ready, listen again, speaking the count as indicated.

a. *Rhythm 1a*: (1 2 3 4)

b. *Rhythm 2a*: (1 2 3 4)

c. *Rhythm 3a*: (1 2 3)

d. *Rhythm 4a*: (1 2 3 4)

e. *Rhythm 5a*: (1 2 3 4)

f. *Rhythm 6a*: (1 2 3 4)

g. *Rhythm 7a*: (1 2 3 4)

Playing and Singing   The exercises below are for playing and singing. They use rhythms you have learned thus far.

For playing, use a piano or another keyboard instrument. A small xylophone is also a good choice. For singing, perform these examples singing the name of each note. We will explore singing with numbers and syllables starting in Chapter Five. You may have to experiment to find the correct range in which to sing each exercise.

9   Play and sing these melodies.

h.

TERMS, SYMBOLS, AND CONCEPTS

𝄽

meter

measure

bar line

strong and weak beats

>

time signatures

counting the basic pulse

metronome

dividing the basic pulse

Chapter Three

Eighth Rest

A silence equal in duration to the eighth note (♪) is the **eighth rest** (♪). We now know four rhythmic symbols:

quarter note: ♩

quarter rest: 𝄽

eighth note: ♪

eighth rest: ♪

Note Values

If the quarter note is the basic pulse, it has a value of one beat. We can then measure other rhythmic symbols against this quarter-note beat.

♩ = 1 beat

𝄽 = 1 beat

♪ = 1/2 beat

♪ = 1/2 beat

1

Giving the quarter a value of one beat, add the total number of beats in each rhythmic pattern.

Example

| ♩ | | 𝄽 | | ♪ | | ♪ | | ♪ | ♪ | ♩ | | ♪ | = 5 1/2 beats |
| 1 | + | 1 | + | 1/2 | + | 1/2 | + | 1/2 | + | 1/2 | + | 1 | + | 1/2 |

a.

𝄽   𝄽   𝄽   𝄽   ♪♪   =

b.

♪ ♪ ♪ ♪ ♪ ♪ ♪ ♪ 𝄽   =

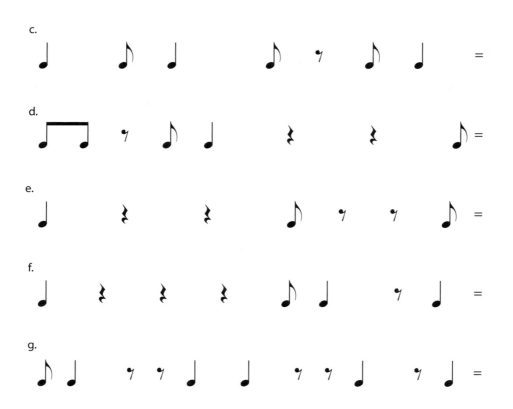

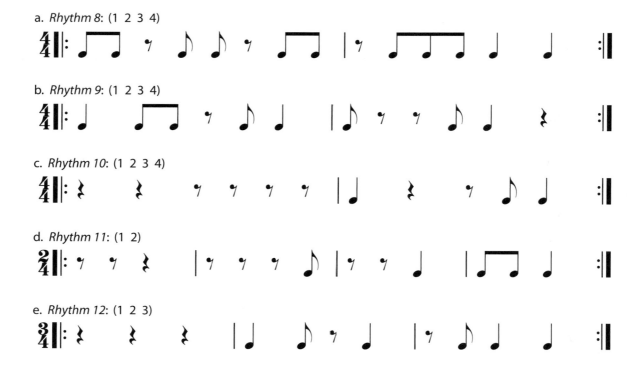

Speaking the Eighth Rest

When speaking rhythms, say the sound "mm" for the eighth rest. When clapping or tapping a rhythm, speak each rest, but don't clap or tap it. Say "rest" for the quarter rest.

2 Speak these rhythms with the CD (tracks 20–24). Do not tap.

a. *Rhythm 8*: (1 2 3 4)

b. *Rhythm 9*: (1 2 3 4)

c. *Rhythm 10*: (1 2 3 4)

d. *Rhythm 11*: (1 2)

e. *Rhythm 12*: (1 2 3)

3   Repeat *Rhythms 8–12*, speaking and tapping. Don't tap the rests, but speak them. Follow the notation in exercise 2, above.

4   Now listen to *Rhythms 8a–12a* (CD, tracks 32–36). Repeat, speaking the count through notes and rests; do not tap. Remember to divide the quarter-note beat with "and," as indicated.

a. *Rhythm 8a*: (1 2 3 4)

b. *Rhythm 9a*: (1 2 3 4)

c. *Rhythm 10a*: (1 2 3 4)

d. *Rhythm 11a*: (1 2)

e. *Rhythm 12a*: (1 2 3)

5   Count and tap the following rhythms, this time dividing each quarter-note beat with "and." Before you start tapping, speak a few measures of the count ("one and two and three and four and" for an exercise in ♩). When the count feels comfortable, add the tapping. Start with a slow tempo. Remember to keep the count steady.

a. Tap:

b. Tap:

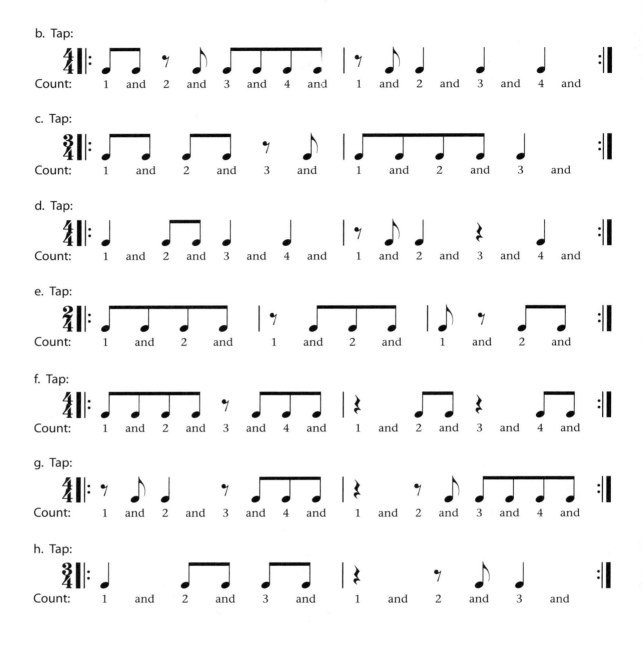

6

Write each of the following rhythms on the Rhythm Spacer. Remember that the eighth rest is equal to the eighth note in duration, and rests are lightly shaded.

a.

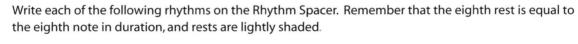

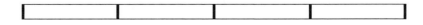

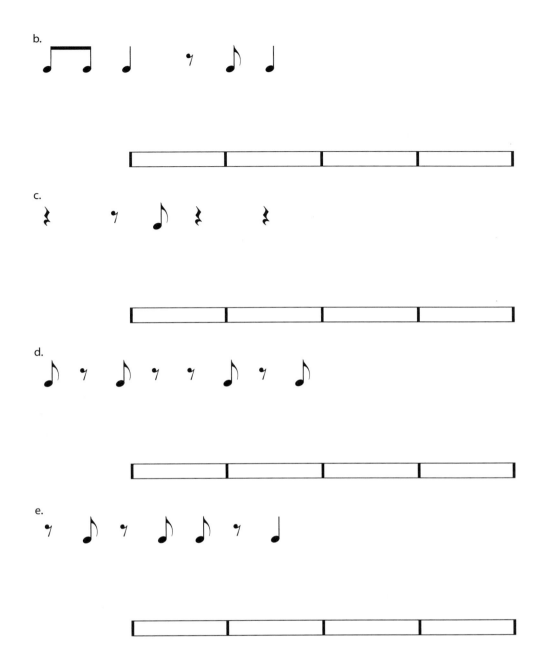

b.

c.

d.

e.

1st and 2nd Endings

When an exercise or piece of music contains repeat signs, you may find two endings. If so, when you repeat, skip the measure or measures marked **1st ending** and go directly to the measure or measures marked **2nd ending**.

Example

This is performed: (1st ending)

(repeat)   (2nd ending)

7 Tap the following rhythms. (Do not tap the rests.)

a.

b.

Other Types of Repeats   **D.C. al fine** (*da capo al fine*) literally means "from the beginning to the end." If you find this abbreviation at the end of a piece, go back to the beginning and repeat, stopping at the place marked *fine* (end).

D.S. (*dal segno*) literally means "from the sign." If you find the letters *D.S.* at the end of a piece, go back to the sign (𝄋), which is not always at the beginning of the piece but sometimes in the middle, and repeat to the end.

8 Play and sing.

a.

b.

c.

9 Tap out the rhythms of the following pieces from the *Scorebook*.

Game Song (*Scorebook* 5)

Brocham Lom (*Scorebook* 10)

TERMS, SYMBOLS, AND CONCEPTS

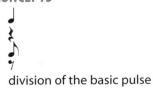

division of the basic pulse

1st and 2nd endings
D.C. al fine
D.S.
𝄋

Chapter Four

Notes Longer Than the Quarter Note

Most of the rhythms we have studied up until now featured the quarter note as the basic pulse. We will now use the quarter note to measure longer notes.

Dotted notes, such as the dotted half note given above, equal the value of the original note (in this instance 2) plus half that value (in this instance 1), for a total of 3. This concept will be explained in more detail in Chapter Five.

1

Listen to *Rhythms 13–16* on the CD (tracks 37–40). The rhythms, notated below, have two parts, and are played on various instruments. The bottom part, which starts the rhythm, gives the quarter-note beat throughout. When you are familiar with each rhythm, tap the top part along with the CD.

a. *Rhythm 13*:

b. *Rhythm 14*:

c. *Rhythm 15*:

d. *Rhythm 16:*

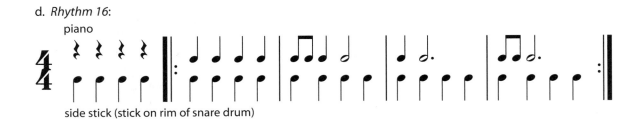

piano

side stick (stick on rim of snare drum)

Rests Longer Than the Quarter Rest

Just as different notes represent different durations of musical sound in time, so do different rests represent different durations of silence. The rests that correspond to the whole note and half note are the following:

whole rest: ▬ = ↕ ↕ ↕ ↕

half rest: ▬ = ↕ ↕

anacrusis (pickup or upbeat) notes before the bar line ✳

2 Tap and count the following rhythms.

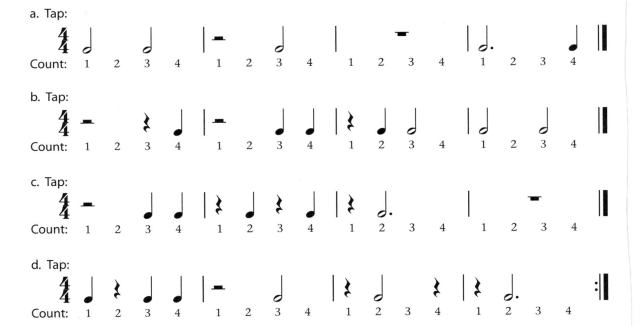

a. Tap:

Count: 1 2 3 4 1 2 3 4 1 2 3 4 1 2 3 4

b. Tap:

Count: 1 2 3 4 1 2 3 4 1 2 3 4 1 2 3 4

c. Tap:

Count: 1 2 3 4 1 2 3 4 1 2 3 4 1 2 3 4

d. Tap:

Count: 1 2 3 4 1 2 3 4 1 2 3 4 1 2 3 4

Anacrusis

Sometimes a piece of music begins in the middle or last part of a measure, before the first downbeat. This partial opening measure is called an **anacrusis** (occasionally a **pickup** or **upbeat**). This practice is common in many songs, including "The Star Spangled Banner."

Oh ___ say can you see, by the etc.

The value of the anacrusis is subtracted from the last measure of the piece. Observe the anacrusis and its effect on the final measure in the following examples:

Counting the Anacrusis There are two ways a performer can count the meter of a piece that begins with an anacrusis. One way is to prepare the downbeat by counting an entire measure and fitting the opening notes where they belong at the end of a measure:

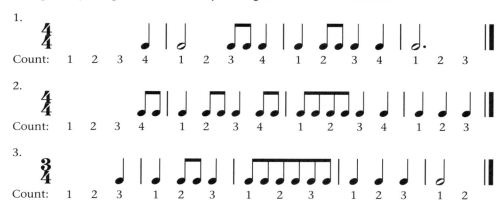

Another way is to "pick up" the count some time after "1" of this imaginary measure, thereby establishing the meter without counting out an entire measure:

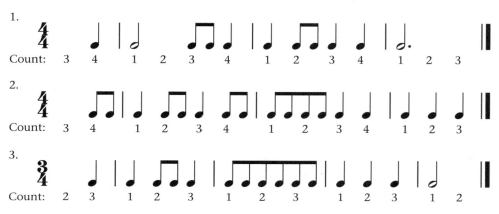

3 Each of the following rhythms contains an anacrusis. Position the notes correctly above the counted numbers. Draw the bar lines *through* the numbers. Tap each rhythm when it is complete. Study the example carefully.

Example

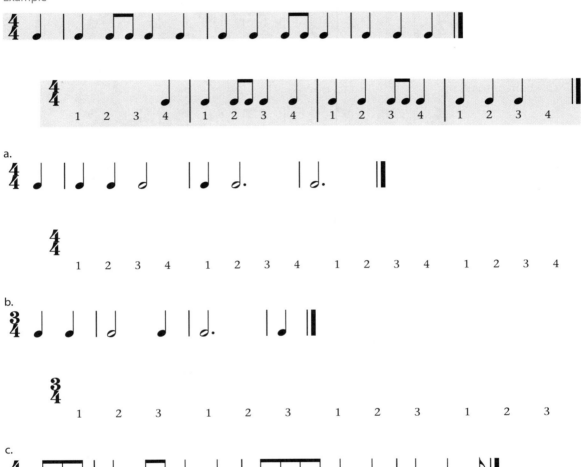

a.

b.

c.

1 and 2 and 3 and 4 and 1 and 2 and 3 and 4 and 1 and 2 and 3 and 4 and 1 and 2 and 3 and 4 and

d.

4 Each of the following rhythms begins with an anacrusis, but the last measure is missing. Make up a rhythm that correctly ends the rhythmic pattern. Remember that the note values of the last measure must complete the meter when added to the anacrusis. Tap each rhythm when it is complete. Study the example carefully.

Example

The one-beat anacrusis in this example requires that the last measure contain two beats. Here are three correct solutions:

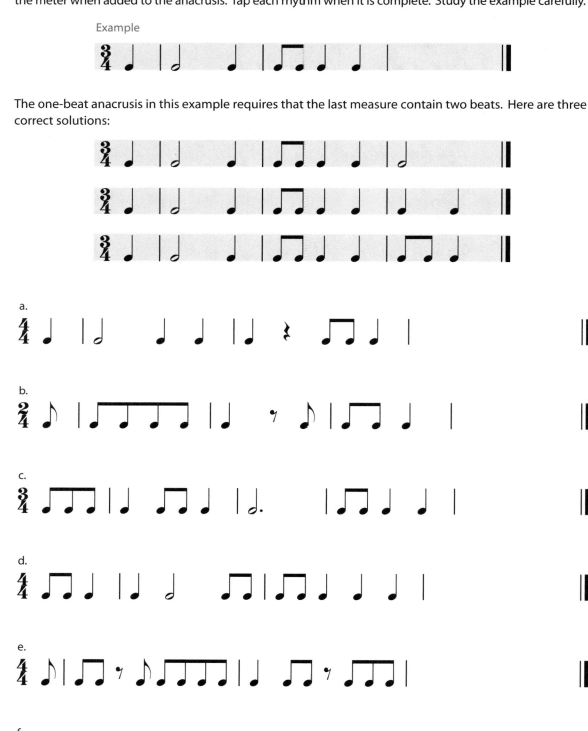

g.

h.

5

Listen to *Rhythms 17–20* on the CD (tracks 41–44). Notice that the lower part of each rhythm provides the basic pulse. When you are familiar with the rhythms, tap the top part along with the recording. Repeat several times.

a. *Rhythm 17*:

b. *Rhythm 18*:

c. *Rhythm 19*:

d. *Rhythm 20*:

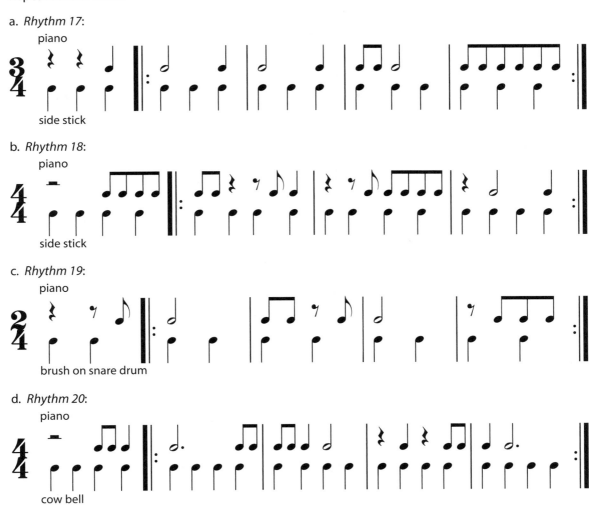

In the rhythms above, you may notice that the upper part looks like an anacrusis, yet the final measure has a full number of beats. This is because the lower part begins on "1," and *both* parts together make up the complete rhythm.

Creating a Drum Pattern

Using the notes we have learned so far, we can create some basic drum patterns that a rock or pop drummer might play. In the following exercises these patterns use a high-hat,* snare drum, and bass drum (called a "kick" drum because it is played with a foot pedal).

6

Listen to Rhythms 21–22 on the CD (tracks 45–46). Repeat each rhythm several times, following the parts separately. Tap each part separately. Finally, listen to the rhythm as a whole, following all three parts at once.

a. *Rhythm 21:*

b. *Rhythm 22:*

Conducting

Some basic conducting patterns, using ♩ as the basic pulse, are given below. By performing them, you will translate each meter into physical action. The lines indicate the motion of the arm led by the hand. The motion should be free and flowing. As you develop the basic movements, count the meter.

7

Perform these basic conducting patterns. Start at the asterisk.

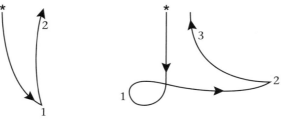

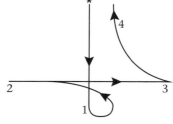

2 basic pulses   3 basic pulses   4 basic pulses

*A pair of small cymbals with a foot pedal that opens and closes them.

8 Tap out the following pieces from the *Scorebook*:

> *Lullaby* (Apache) (*Scorebook* 11)
>
> *Fray Diego* (*Scorebook* 4)
>
> *O du schöner Rosengarten* (*Scorebook* 12)
>
> *Oliver and the Maiden* (*Scorebook* 7)
>
> *Die Gedanken sind frei* (*Scorebook* 18)
>
> *Oh How Lovely Is the Evening* (*Scorebook* 58)
>
> *Come, Let Us Tune* (*Scorebook* 1)
>
> *Das walt' Gott Vater und Gott Sohn* (*Scorebook* 3)
>
> *Music in the Air* (*Scorebook* 14)
>
> *Repentance* (*Scorebook* 15)

9 Play and sing the following melodies.

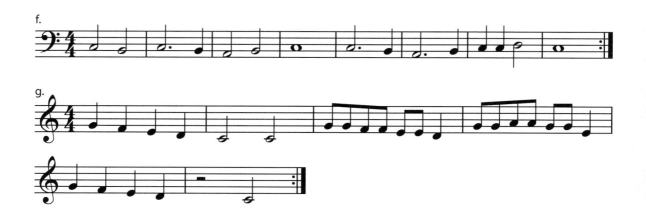

f.

g.

TERMS, SYMBOLS, AND CONCEPTS

anacrusis
conducting patterns

Chapter Five

Note System

This chapter presents the basic symbols for rhythm in the Western notation system. Unlike the symbols presented in previous chapters, many of the ones you learn in this chapter will not be used in performing exercises. Instead, focus on the way each symbol fits into the notation system—that is, how its duration relates to the other notes or rests in this system.

Dividing the Whole Note

In our notation system, the whole note may be divided into smaller notes. The symbol for each note and its equivalent rest is presented below. The duration of each note or rest in this list is *half the duration* of the note or rest above it.

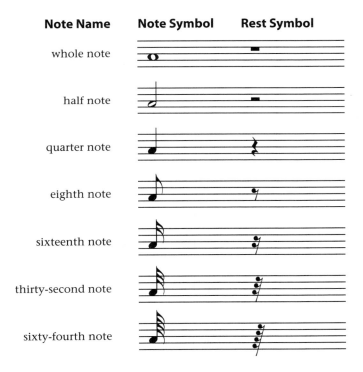

Note Name	Note Symbol	Rest Symbol
whole note		
half note		
quarter note		
eighth note		
sixteenth note		
thirty-second note		
sixty-fourth note		

Another way of presenting the relationship among the notes given in the chart above appears below. Notice that each note has the same durations as *two* of the notes directly below it:

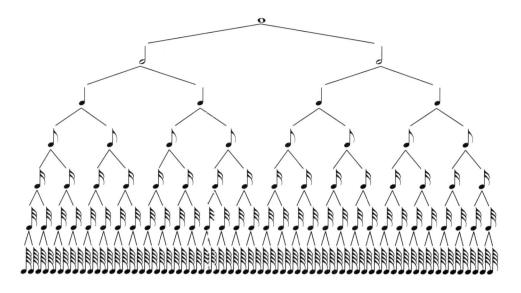

Beams

Notes smaller than the quarter note are written with flags (♪ ♫ ♬). When a group of flagged notes are written together, unifying beams are used.

Notice that the number of flags is replaced by the same number of beams.

Combinations of Notes with Beams

Notes of different time values can be joined together with beams when they all occur within the same beat.

The beam may be on the left or right side of the note stem. It is the number of beams that touch the stem that determines the value of the note.

1 Rewrite these rhythms with flags.

Example

a.

 =

b.

=

c.

=

d.

=

Relationship of Note Values

As we have discovered, the quarter note is often used as the basic unit for measuring the values of other notes. Below, each note is expressed in quarter notes.

1. Notes larger than the quarter note:

2. Notes smaller than the quarter note are often beamed in groups equal to one quarter note in duration:

2   Write the number of smaller-value notes that equal the indicated larger-value note.

Example

𝅝 = (in 𝅗𝅥) 𝅗𝅥 𝅗𝅥

a.

𝅗𝅥. = (in 𝅘𝅥)

b.

𝅗𝅥 = (in 𝅘𝅥)

c.

𝅘𝅥 = (in 𝅘𝅥𝅮)

d.

𝅗𝅥 = (in 𝅘𝅥𝅮)

e.

𝅝 = (in 𝅘𝅥𝅮)

f.

𝅗𝅥 = (in 𝅘𝅥𝅯)

g.

𝅗𝅥. = (in 𝅘𝅥𝅮)

h.

𝅗𝅥. = (in 𝅘𝅥𝅯)

i

𝅗𝅥 = (in 𝅘𝅥𝅯)

The Tie

Two notes of the same pitch may be connected with a curved line joining one note-head to the other. This line is called a **tie**. The first note is then prolonged by the value of the second. (The second is not played.)

tied notes		number of quarter-note beats
𝅗𝅥 ⌣ 𝅘𝅥	=	3
𝅗𝅥 ⌣ 𝅗𝅥	=	4
𝅘𝅥 ⌣ 𝅘𝅥	=	2
𝅝 ⌣ 𝅘𝅥	=	5

Ties and Slurs

Do not confuse the tie with a similar curved line called the **slur**, which indicates that two or more *different* pitches are to be played smoothly (see *Workbook*, Appendixes I, VII). The tie always joins two notes of the same pitch.

Ties

Slurs

The Dotted Note

We have already learned about one dotted note, the dotted half note (♩.). But any note can be dotted. A dot after a note lengthens the note by half its own value. Notice that prolonging a note with the addition of a dot is an alternative to using a tie to accomplish the same purpose.

The dot is *always* placed in a space, even when the note it augments falls on a line. For example:

3

With the quarter note valued at one beat, give the numerical value of each of these notes or groups of notes.

Examples

a.

𝅝· =

f.

=

b.

=

g.

=

c.

=

h.

=

d.

=

i.

=

e.

=

j.

𝅝· 𝅗𝅥· =

---

4 Write one note that equals each of these rhythmic groupings.

Example

a.

=

e.

=

b.

=

f.

=

c.

=

g.

=

d.

=

h.

=

i.

=

5 Name each symbol and give its value, with the quarter note valued at one beat.

6 Give the total of each rhythmic group, with the quarter note valued at one beat.

Example

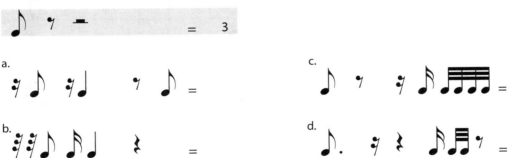

= 3

a.

b.

c.

d.

Writing Rests When writing rests, musicians follow certain practices that differ from the way notes are written.

1. The whole rest (▬) may represent a full measure of rest *in any meter.* It always hangs beneath the *fourth* line of the staff in the *center* of the measure.

Example

2. Rests are not tied.

3. Half rests (▬) always sit atop the third line. They are rarely used in ⅜.

4. Quarter rests (𝄾) and half rests (▬) are usually written on the beat, not in between the beats.

7

Play and sing the following melodies. Examine the section on singing major-scale melodies in the *Workbook* (pp. 89–90) as well as the methods for sight singing given in Supplementary Guide I, pp. 273–276 of the *Workbook*. Write either numbers or syllables, or both, below each note before you perform each melody. The first two melodies are done for you; (a) uses numbers, (b) uses syllables.

8 Choose melodies from the following to sing with numbers or syllables.

John Hatton, *Come, Let Us Tune* (*Scorebook* 1)

J. S. Bach, Chorale Melody from *Christmas Oratorio* (*Scorebook* 2)

Das walt' Gott Vater und Gott Sohn (*Scorebook* 3)

Fray Diego (*Scorebook* 4)

Game Song (*Scorebook* 5)

Den Vater dort oben (*Scorebook* 6)

Oliver and the Maiden (*Scorebook* 7)

TERMS, SYMBOLS, AND CONCEPTS

notation system
beam
flag
tie
slur
dotted note

Chapter Six

Working with Ties and Dotted Notes

Rhythms that feature tied or dotted notes require special attention when related to the basic pulse. Observe the positions of the following tied or dotted notes on the Rhythm Spacer:

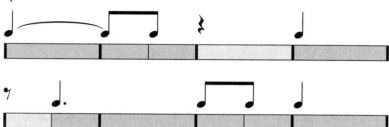

1 ....

Write each of the following rhythms on the provided Rhythm Spacer, as in the example above.

a.

b.

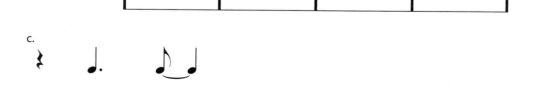

c.

d.

e.

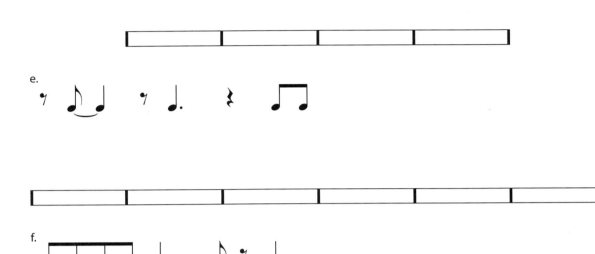

f.

2 Listen to *Rhythms 23–26* on the CD (tracks 47–50). Notice that the lower notated part provides the basic pulse. When you are familiar with the rhythms, tap the *top part only* with the recording.

a. *Rhythm 23*:

piano

bass drum

b. *Rhythm 24*:

kalimba

shaker

c. *Rhythm 25*:

piano

claves

d. *Rhythm 26*:

piano

bass drum

Division of the Basic Pulse

Counting the basic pulse with the "one and two and" method can help you understand how to perform tied or dotted rhythms. Observe the division of the basic pulse in the following examples:

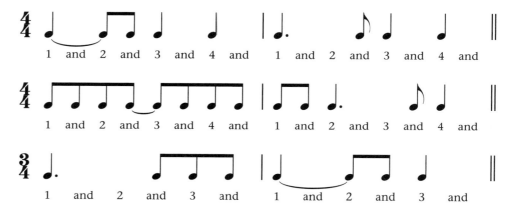

3

Position each of the following rhythms above the divided pulse, as in the examples above. Tap each rhythm as you count it.

a.

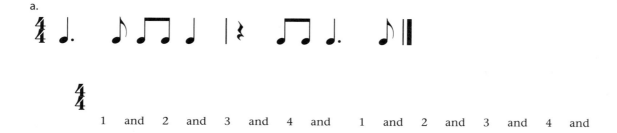

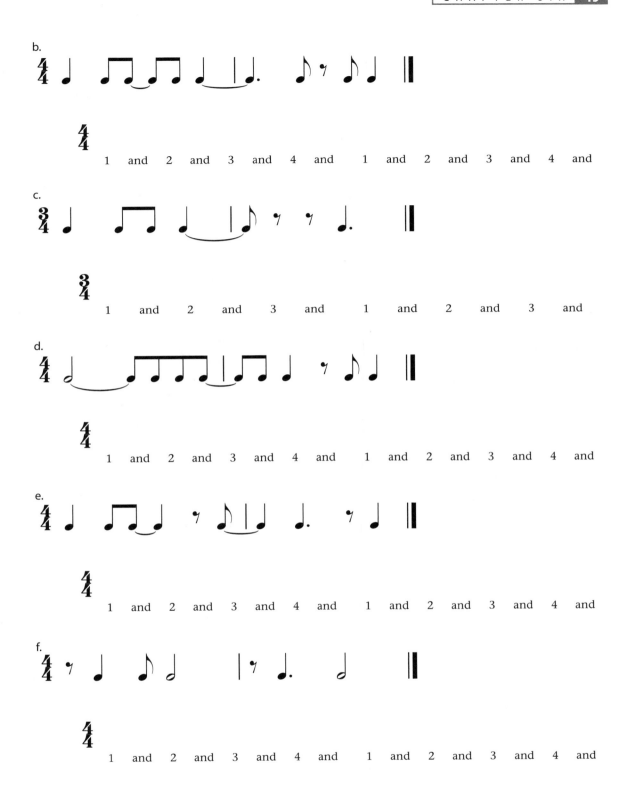

Coordinating Both Hands

Until now, we have tapped and counted one part at a time. Now we will begin tapping two parts simultaneously. Not only will this process help you understand certain rhythms, it will also help to give you the coordination necessary to play many musical instruments.

4 Tap the following rhythms separately.

a. Use the right hand:

b. Use the left hand:

5 a. Now tap with both hands at once. Tap eighth notes with the right hand against quarters with the left:

right hand

left hand

b. Repeat with the parts reversed:

right hand

left hand

6 Tap these rhythms. First start the left hand *alone*. When you have established the basic pulse, *add* the right hand.

a. Tap:

right hand

left hand

b.

right hand

left hand

c.

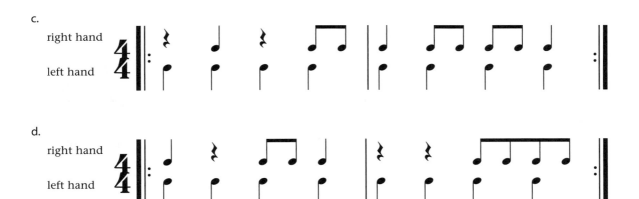

d.

7

Tap *Rhythms 13–16* with the CD (tracks 37–40), using both hands.

a. *Rhythm 13*:

b. *Rhythm 14*:

c. *Rhythm 15*:

d. *Rhythm 16*:

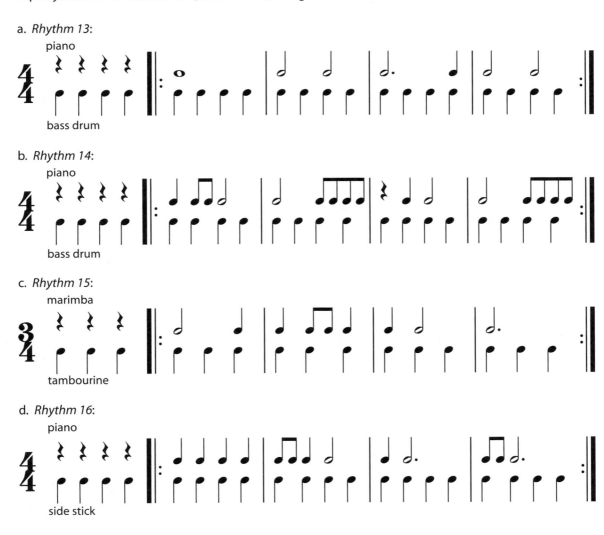

8 Tap the following rhythms using both hands.

a.

right hand
left hand

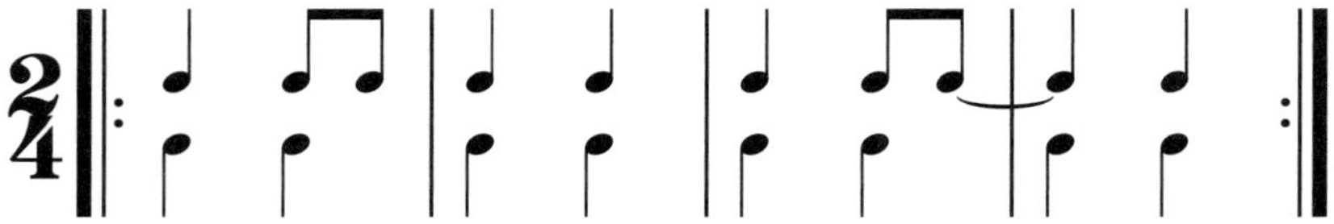

b.

right hand
left hand

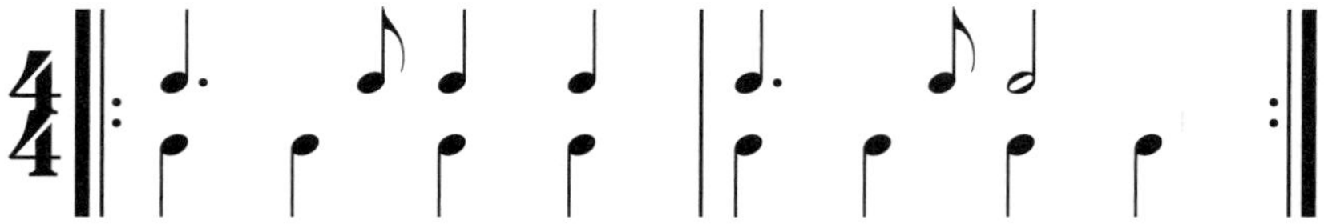

c.

right hand
left hand

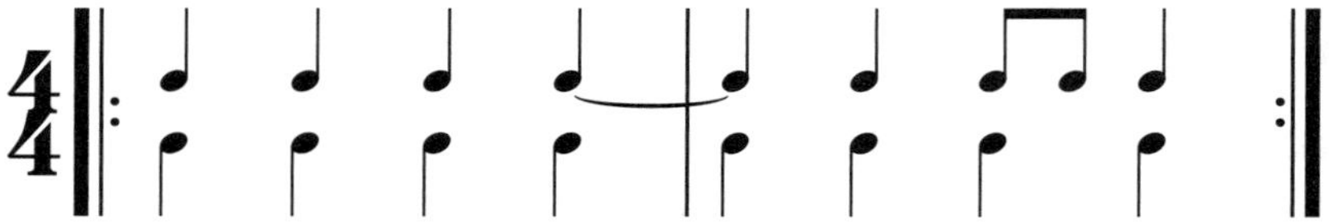

d.

right hand
left hand

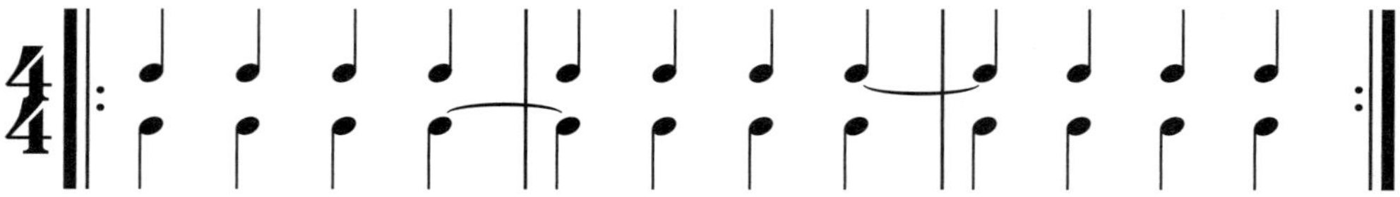

e.

right hand
left hand

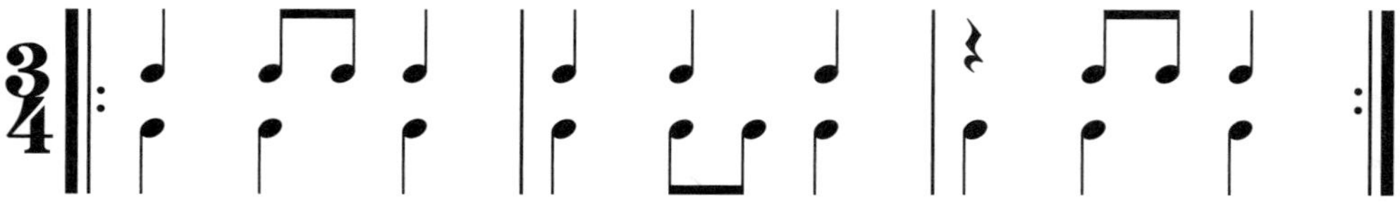

Marking the Beat

Musicians often use a type of shorthand to "mark the beat"—that is, to keep track of where beats fall within the rhythmic structure of a piece. In the following examples, small lines are drawn where every quarter-note pulse occurs:

quarter-note beat

quarter-note beat

9 Mark small lines where each quarter-note beat falls.

Example

10 Tap the rhythms from the following *Scorebook* pieces:

Cradle Song (*Scorebook* 40)

O'er the Burn, Bessie (*Scorebook* 41)

The Hunter (*Scorebook* 24)

Dona nobis pacem (*Scorebook* 57)

Beethoven, "Ode to Joy" theme from Symphony No. 9 (*Scorebook* 9)

Mozart, Theme from *Don Giovanni* (*Scorebook* 76)

Morley, *Nancie* (*Scorebook* 75)

Just As I Am (*Scorebook* 8)

Henry Martin (*Scorebook* 55)

11 Play and sing the following exercises. Use numbers or syllables when you sing.

12 Choose from the following melodies and sing.

Bradbury, *Just As I Am* (*Scorebook* 8)

Beethoven, "Ode to Joy" theme from Symphony No. 9 (*Scorebook* 9)

Music in the Air (*Scorebook* 14)

Coles, *Repentance* (*Scorebook* 15)

The Water Is Wide (*Scorebook* 46)

Barbrie Allen (*Scorebook* 47)

Amazing Grace (*Scorebook* 50)

TERMS, SYMBOLS, AND CONCEPTS

counting ties and dotted notes
two-hand coordination
marking the beat

Chapter Seven

Subdivision of the Quarter Note into Sixteenth Notes

The quarter note can be subdivided into four parts with the use of sixteenth notes. The symbol for a sixteenth note is a ♪. Notice that it has two flags (or two beams) on its stem. When speaking the following patterns, accent "one" in each group of four.

1 Tap the following rhythms, speaking the count at a moderate to fast tempo.

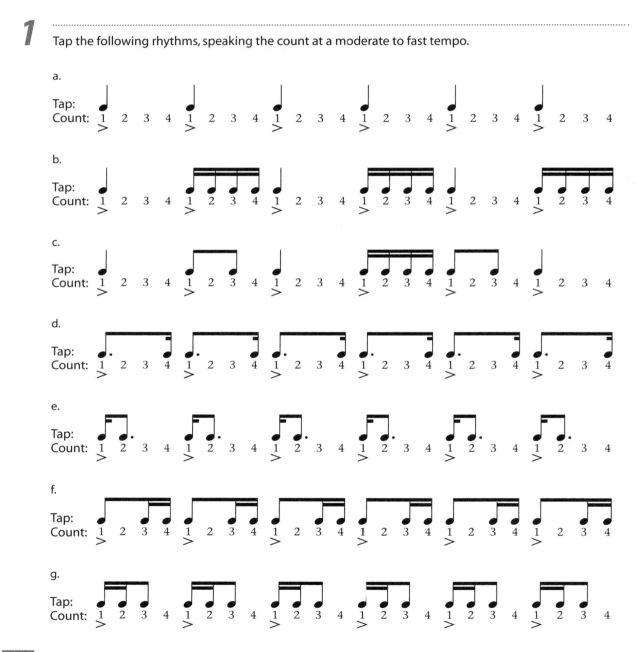

h.

Tap:
Count: 1 2 3 4 1 2 3 4 1 2 3 4 1 2 3 4 1 2 3 4 1 2 3 4
      >   >   >   >   >   >

2 Rewrite the rhythms found in exercise 1 below the subdivisions. Write the stems down.

a.
 >   >   >   >   >   >
1 2 3 4 1 2 3 4 1 2 3 4 1 2 3 4 1 2 3 4 1 2 3 4

b.
 >   >   >   >   >   >
1 2 3 4 1 2 3 4 1 2 3 4 1 2 3 4 1 2 3 4 1 2 3 4

c.
 >   >   >   >   >   >
1 2 3 4 1 2 3 4 1 2 3 4 1 2 3 4 1 2 3 4 1 2 3 4

d.
 >   >   >   >   >   >
1 2 3 4 1 2 3 4 1 2 3 4 1 2 3 4 1 2 3 4 1 2 3 4

e.
 >   >   >   >   >   >
1 2 3 4 1 2 3 4 1 2 3 4 1 2 3 4 1 2 3 4 1 2 3 4

f.
 >   >   >   >   >   >
1 2 3 4 1 2 3 4 1 2 3 4 1 2 3 4 1 2 3 4 1 2 3 4

g.
 >   >   >   >   >   >
1 2 3 4 1 2 3 4 1 2 3 4 1 2 3 4 1 2 3 4 1 2 3 4

h.
 >   >   >   >   >   >
1 2 3 4 1 2 3 4 1 2 3 4 1 2 3 4 1 2 3 4 1 2 3 4

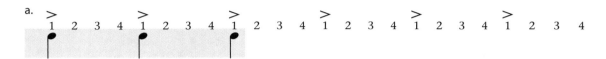

3 Listen to *Rhythms 27–32* on the CD (tracks 51–56). Repeat several times. When you are familiar with the rhythms, tap the upper part only.

a. *Rhythm 27*:

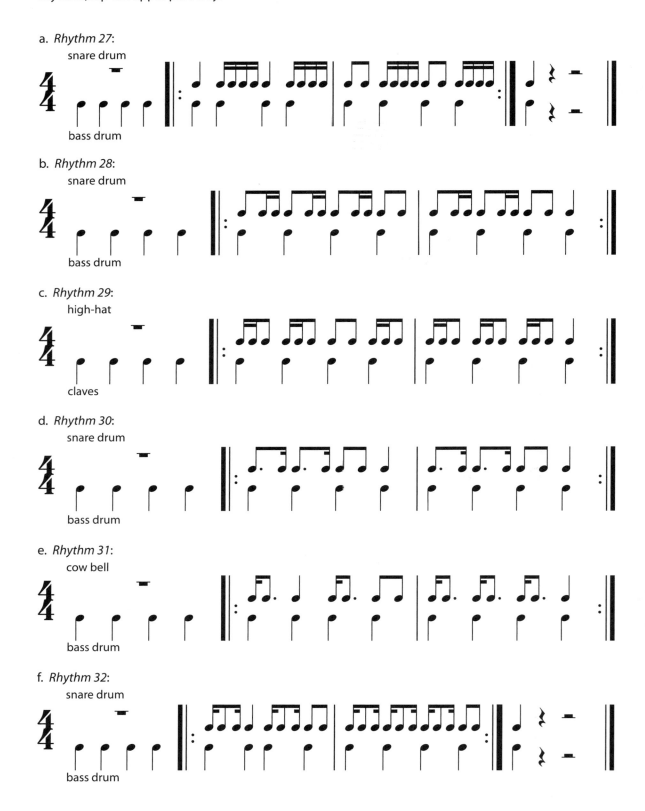

b. *Rhythm 28*:

c. *Rhythm 29*:

d. *Rhythm 30*:

e. *Rhythm 31*:

f. *Rhythm 32*:

***Speaking Sixteenth
Notes in Meter***

When subdividing into sixteenth notes within a metered rhythm that uses the quarter note as the basic beat, the sixteenth notes can be counted in this way: "one ee and a" (spoken slurred together, with the accent on "one").

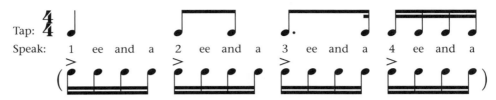

This method helps you keep track of the beat within the measure while still subdividing each beat into four parts.

4

Tap the following rhythms while counting "1ee and a" for each beat.

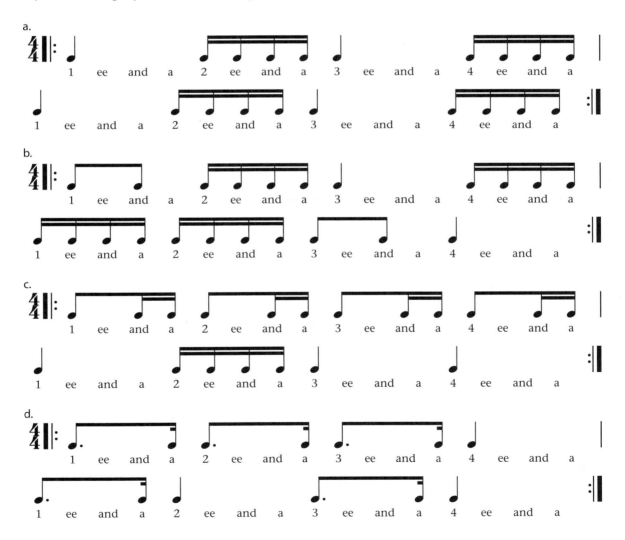

5 Write each of the following rhythms above the divided pulse. Tap each rhythm slowly while speaking the count.

a.

1 ee and a   2 ee and a   3 ee and a   4 ee and a

b.

1 ee and a   2 ee and a   3 ee and a   4 ee and a

c.

1 ee and a   2 ee and a   3 ee and a   4 ee and a

d.

1 ee and a   2 ee and a   3 ee and a   4 ee and a

6 Listen to *Rhythms 33–36* on the CD (tracks 57–60). Repeat several times. When you are familiar with the rhythms, tap the upper part.

a. *Rhythm 33*:

b. *Rhythm 34*:

c. *Rhythm 35*:

d. *Rhythm 36*:

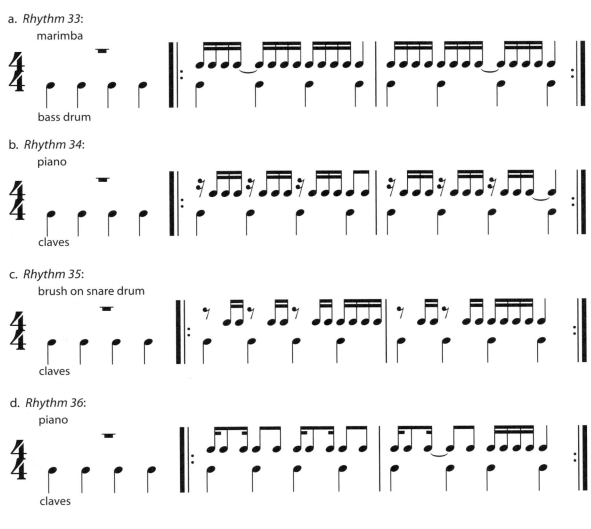

7 Tap with both hands.

a.

b.

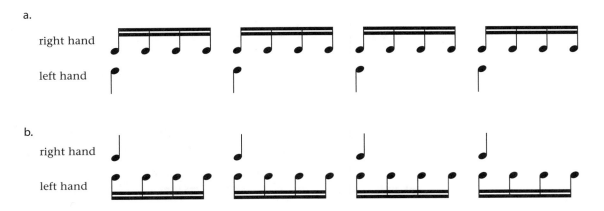

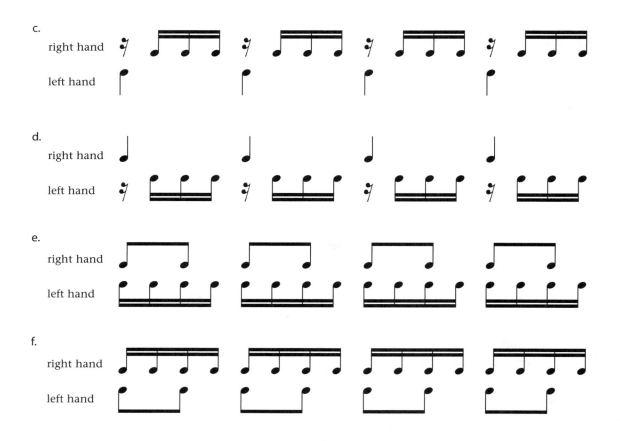

c.

d.

e.

f.

8 Tap the following exercises with both hands. Practice each part separately before you combine them.

a.

b.

c.

d.

right hand

left hand

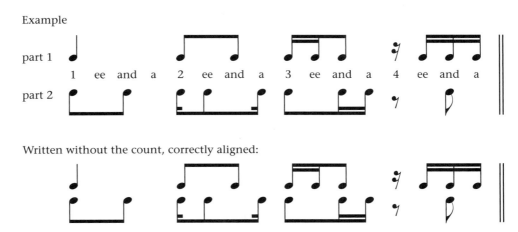

Aligning Two or More Parts

Notes that sound together are written directly above or below each other. The correct spacing of two or more separate parts shows exactly where the notes occur, as on p. 30. In the following exercises, in two parts, align each rhythm with the count. Then rewrite the two rhythms without the count. Study the example carefully.

Example

part 1

1   ee   and   a   2   ee   and   a   3   ee   and   a   4   ee   and   a

part 2

Written without the count, correctly aligned:

9 Write each rhythm with the count that is given. Write part 1 above the count and part 2 below the count. Then copy the two parts again, without the count and correctly aligned, as in the example given above.

a.

part 1   part 2

part 1

1   ee   and   a   2   ee   and   a   3   ee   and   a   4   ee   and   a

part 2

part 1

part 2

b.

part 1  part 2

part 1

1   ee   and   a   2   ee   and   a   3   ee   and   a   4   ee   and   a

part 2

part 1

part 2

10 Tap the following pieces from the *Scorebook*.

> *Jeune fillete* (*Scorebook* 34)
>
> *Carraig Aonair* (*Scorebook* 26)
>
> *The Knife Sharpener* (*Scorebook* 29)
>
> Hymn (Armenian) (*Scorebook* 44)
>
> *The Oak and the Ash* (*Scorebook* 54)
>
> *Robin Adair* (*Scorebook* 16)

11 Sing the following exercises. For (a), (b), and (c), which use the first five notes of parallel major and minor keys, use the numbers provided. For the others, write numbers, syllables, or both before you sing. See Supplementary Guide I of the *Workbook*, page 273.

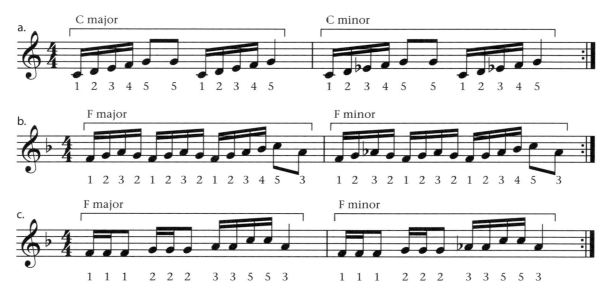

d. D minor

e. C minor

f. G minor

g. E minor

12 Choose from among the following melodies and sing:

The Trees They Do Grow High (Scorebook 22)

In dem Weiten stand ein Haus (Scorebook 25)

Que ne suis-je la fougère (Scorebook 27)

Dear Willie (Scorebook 52)

Hey, Ho, Nobody at Home (Scorebook 59)

The Welcome Song (Scorebook 60)

TERMS, SYMBOLS, AND CONCEPTS

subdivision of the quarter note
counting sixteenths

aligning two or more parts

Chapter Eight

**Simple and
Compound Meters**

All of the meters we have studied so far feature a basic pulse that is divided into two; such a meter is called a **simple meter**. There are also meters whose basic pulse regularly divides into three parts; such a meter is called a **compound meter**.

Simple Meters

Compound Meters

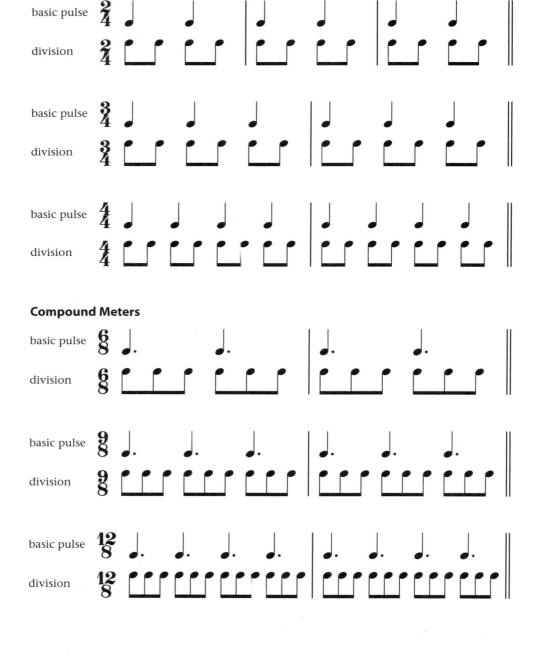

Counting Compound Meter

The simple meters we have encountered have used the quarter note as the basic pulse. With compound meters, the dotted quarter note is most often the basic pulse. Methods for counting compound meters vary depending upon which meter is being counted and at what tempo. For example, $\frac{6}{8}$, one of the most common compound meters, can be counted in the following ways:

Ways to Count $\frac{6}{8}$

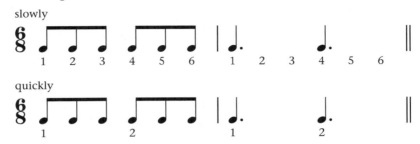

The first example emphasizes the eighth-note divisions of the basic pulse (which is what the time signature indicates to us) and is used mainly for slow tempos. The second example emphasizes the basic pulse and is used for moderate to quick tempos.

1 Tap and count these rhythms.

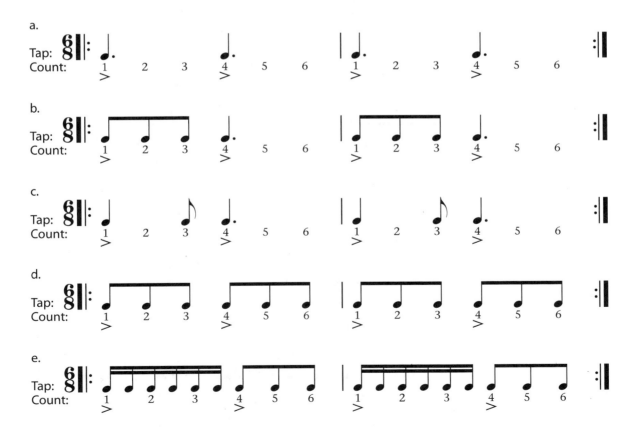

2 Tap and count these rhythms. First tap the left hand. Then add the counting, and then add the right hand.

a.

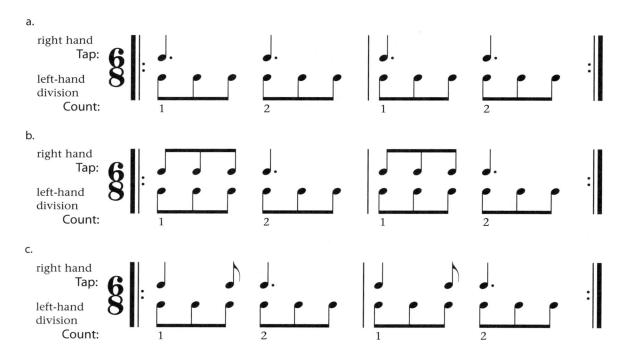

b.

c.

3 Tap the first rhythmic figure of *Silent Night* (*Scorebook* 68) with your right hand against even eighth notes tapped with your left. Singing it will help. Repeat until you have the rhythm right.

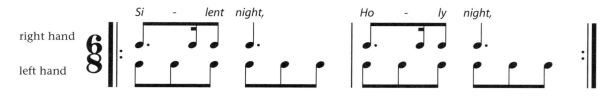

4 Listen to *Rhythms 37–41* (CD, tracks 61–65). After you are familiar with them, tap the top parts only with the recording. Add the left hand when you feel ready.

a. *Rhythm 37*:

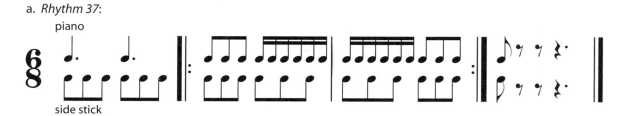

b. *Rhythm 38*:

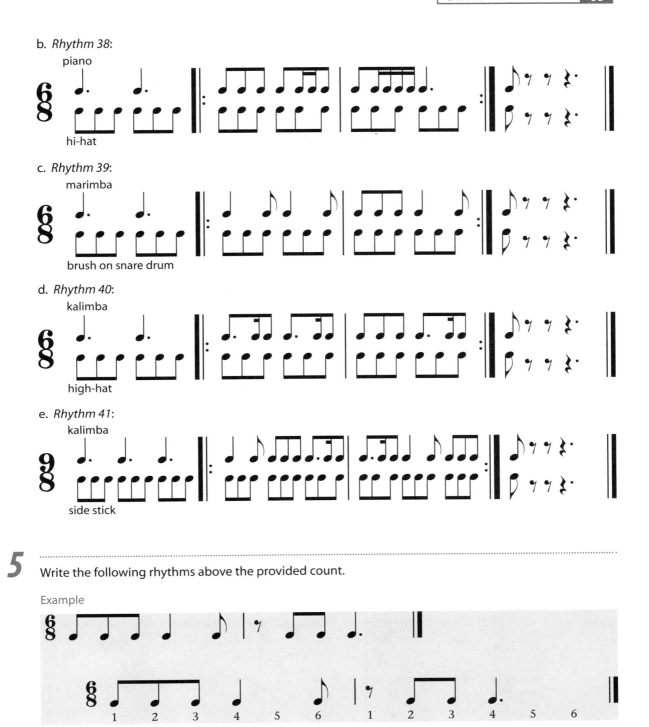

c. *Rhythm 39*:

d. *Rhythm 40*:

e. *Rhythm 41*:

5 Write the following rhythms above the provided count.

Example

a.

b.

c.

d.

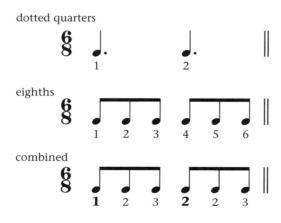

6

Repeat *Rhythms 37–40* (pp. 64–65) with the CD. Count the basic pulse out loud using "1 2 3 4 5 6." Notice that you count eighth notes, not sixteenth notes. Begin counting at the double bar. When you are comfortable with the count, tap the top part while speaking.

Speaking Compound Meter

Here is another method for counting compound meters that can help you keep track of the rhythm within the measure. This method combines the two ways to count compound meter given on p. 63: the first counting eighths (♩♩♩) and the second counting the dotted quarter (♩.).

dotted quarters

eighths

combined

In $\frac{9}{8}$ this count would appear like this:

In $\frac{12}{8}$ the count would be this:

7 Write a count under each of the following rhythms as indicated. Underline the dotted quarter-note pulse.

Example

8 Listen to *Rhythms 42–44* (CD, tracks 66–68). When you are ready, tap the top part. Repeat the rhythms and add a count. You may use any method described so far.

a. *Rhythm 42*:

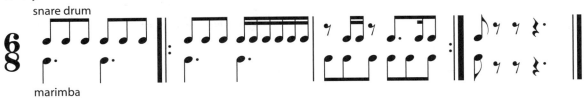

b. *Rhythm 43:*

snare drum

kalimba

c. *Rhythm 44:*

high-hat

kalimba

9 Tap the following pieces from the *Scorebook.*

> *Drink to Me Only with Thine Eyes* (*Scorebook* 48)
>
> *Believe Me If All Those Endearing Young Charms* (*Scorebook* 49)
>
> *Greensleeves* (*Scorebook* 56)
>
> *Drei Reiter um Tor* (*Scorebook* 19)

10 Sing the following exercises.

a. A minor

b. E major

c. B minor

d. B♭ major

e. G minor

f. C minor

g. E minor

11 Choose from the following melodies and sing.

Drink to Me Only with Thine Eyes (*Scorebook* 48)

Drei Reiter um Tor (*Scorebook* 19)

Believe Me If All Those Endearing Young Charms (*Scorebook* 49)

Silent Night (*Scorebook* 68)

TERMS, SYMBOLS, AND CONCEPTS

simple meter

compound meter

basic pulse in compound meter

counting in compound meters

Chapter Nine

Triplets

Any note can be divided into three equal parts. Such a division is called a **triplet**. In this chapter, we will consider the triplet division of the quarter note, which is notated . Notice how the triplets line up with quarter notes.

---

1 Tap the top part of *Rhythm 45* with the CD (track 69). The top part is played by a tambourine, the bottom part by a woodblock. When you are comfortable with the rhythm, tap both parts together.

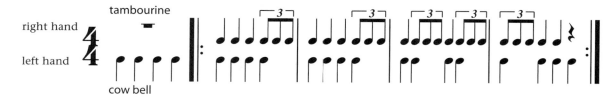

Triplets and Eighth Notes

The use of triplets in a simple meter such as 4/4 allows the quarter note to be divided into three parts as well as two. It is essential to understand the relationship between the normal eighth note and the triplet made out of eighth notes. This difference between the two is demonstrated on the Rhythm Spacer below.

Observe how triplets are aligned on the Rhythm Spacer:

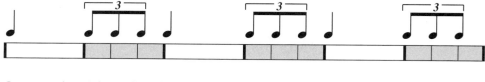

Compare the triplet with eighth notes:

Notice that only the use of a bracket and the number *3* (⌐——3——⌐) distinguishes eighth notes from triplets.

2 Align each pair of rhythms on the Rhythm Spacer, as indicated. You need not use shading.

Example

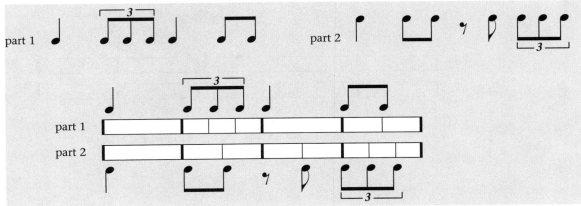

a.

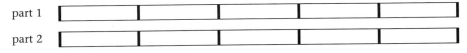

b.

c.

part 1

part 2

part 1					

part 2					

3 Tap the top part of *Rhythm 46* (CD, track 70). Listen to the difference between eighth notes and triplets. When you are comfortable with the rhythm, tap both parts.

right hand

left hand

high-hat

synthesizer

right hand

left hand

Speaking Triplets

The quarter note is divided into *two* equal parts by counting "one and two and." The quarter note can be divided into *three* equal parts by counting "one trip-let, two trip-let," etc., as in the example below.

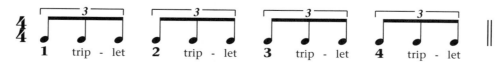

4 Repeat *Rhythm 46* (CD, track 70). Tap and speak the top rhythm, as indicated.

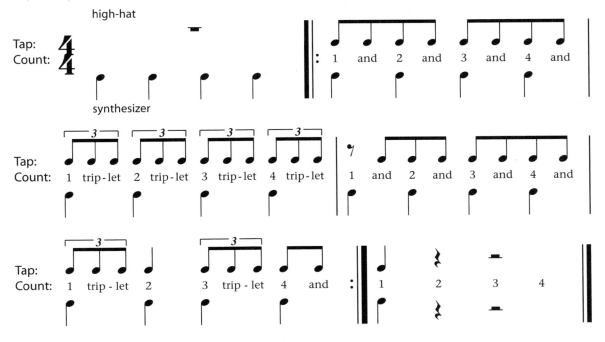

5 Tap the top part of *Rhythm 47* with the CD (track 71). Then tap the bottom part.

The Triplet Rest   When a rest occurs within a triplet, it is written like the eighth rest, but included within the triplet bracket.

6 Tap and count the following exercises.

a.

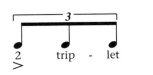

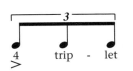

b.

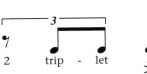

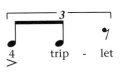

c.

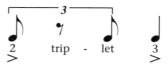
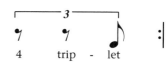

The Triplet and the Basic Pulse

In Chapter Eight, we learned how to count three eighth notes per beat in compound meter. There is an important difference between these eighth notes and the triplets discussed above. The difference lies in the basic pulse. If the meter is compound and the basic pulse is a dotted quarter, a natural division of three eighth notes occurs without special notation. However, when the basic pulse is a quarter note, the triplet bracket is needed in order to signify a three-part division.

Compare:

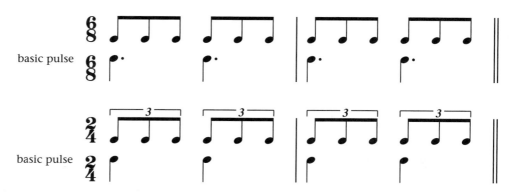

basic pulse

basic pulse

Counting Eighths, Triplets, and Sixteenths

There are many ways to count rhythms. The methods used in this book are not the only ones, but they are often used by students. The idea behind them is that *different* words represent *different* types of rhythmic groupings, such as in the rhythm of exercise 7.

7

Listen to *Rhythms 48–49* (CD, tracks 72–73). When you are familiar with the rhythms, count as indicated and tap. The indication "4x" in *Rhythm 48* means repeat four times.

a. *Rhythm 48*:

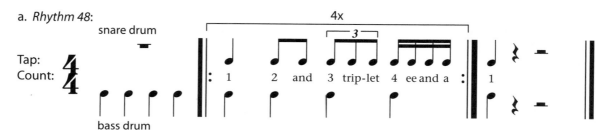

b. *Rhythm 49*:

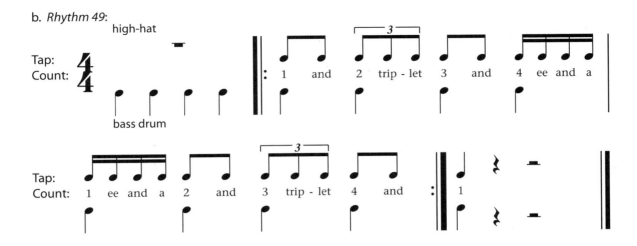

8 Listen to *Rhythms 50* and *51* on the CD (tracks 74–75). In these drum patterns, triplets and sixteenths are used to enhance the basic beat. The indication "toms" refers to tom-toms, drums found in various sizes in a drum set. When you know the rhythm, tap the high-hat and tom-tom parts with the recording. Each rhythm repeats *four* times.

a. *Rhythm 50*:

b. *Rhythm 51*:

9 Tap the following pieces from the *Scorebook*.

La paloma (*Scorebook* 53)

Mozart, Minuet (top part only) (*Scorebook* 80)

10

Sing the following exercises.

g. E minor

h. D minor

11 Choose from the following and sing:

La paloma (*Scorebook* 53)

Brocham Lom (*Scorebook* 10)

The Knife Sharpener (*Scorebook* 29)

Tyler Street (*Scorebook* 35)

Feinsliebchen (*Scorebook* 33)

TERMS, SYMBOLS, AND CONCEPTS

triplet

⌐ *3* ⌐

triplet rest

triplet and the basic pulse

Chapter Ten

Different Values of the Basic Pulse

In the rhythms studied so far, the basic pulse has been ♩ or ♩. Other note values can represent the basic pulse, depending on the tempo, the historical period in which a piece was composed, or the intention of the composer. Observe these examples:

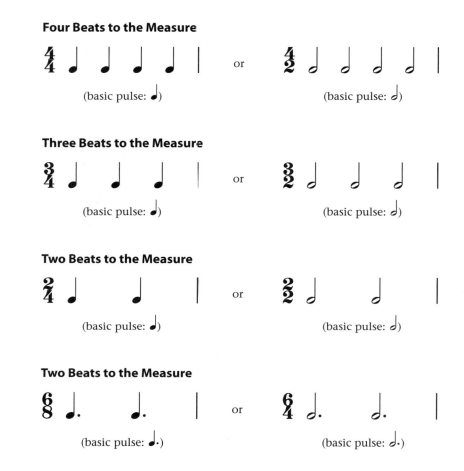

Four Beats to the Measure

(basic pulse: ♩)   or   (basic pulse: ♩)

Three Beats to the Measure

(basic pulse: ♩)   or   (basic pulse: ♩)

Two Beats to the Measure

(basic pulse: ♩)   or   (basic pulse: ♩)

Two Beats to the Measure

(basic pulse: ♩.)   or   (basic pulse: ♩.)

C and ₵

The symbol **C** represents common time, or ⁴⁄₄. The fact that it's called common time indicates the frequency with which this time signature is used. The symbol **₵** (the *alla breve* sign) is equal to ²⁄₂ meter and indicates that the basic number of beats per measure is halved, while the unit of pulse is doubled.

You can make the ratio of note values smaller as well as larger, as illustrated by this example:

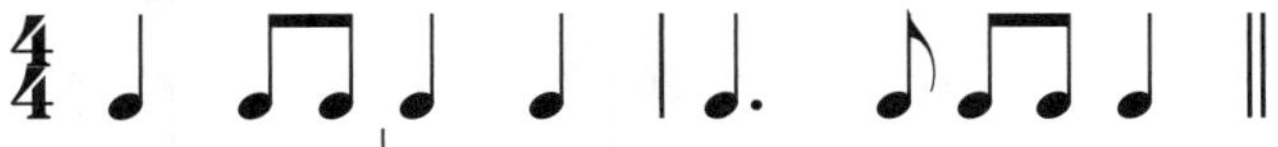

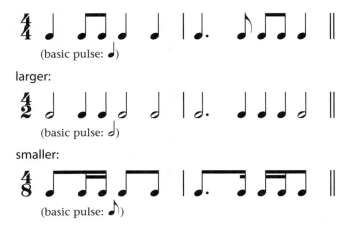

(basic pulse: ♩)

larger:

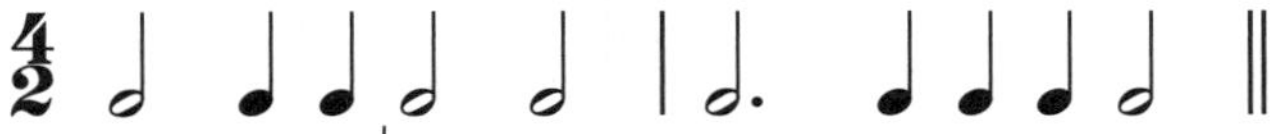

(basic pulse: 𝅗𝅥)

smaller:

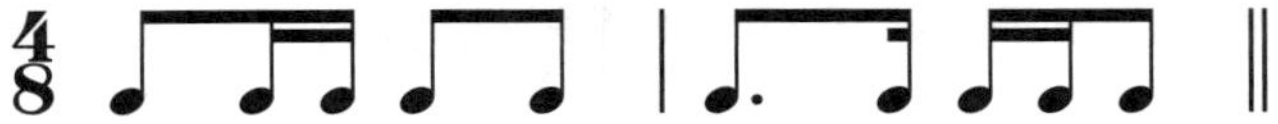

(basic pulse: ♪)

All three rhythms sound exactly alike, if the tempo of the basic pulse is the same. Notice that the second rhythm is created by doubling the original quarter-note pulse, while the third divides the original quarter-note pulse in half.

Double Whole Note and Rest

Rhythms that use the half note as the basic pulse and have four beats per measure may require the use of a **double whole note** or its equivalent rest, the **double whole rest**. The double whole rest, used in $\frac{4}{2}$, is the only exception to the rule of using the normal whole rest (▬) to indicate a measure of silence in any meter. The values of this note and rest are:

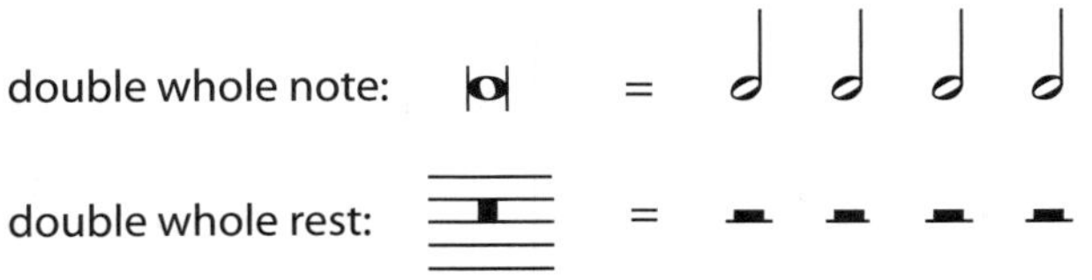

1 Tap *Rhythm 13* with the CD (track 37), first in its original form, then in the other two versions. Study the relationship among the three examples.

a.

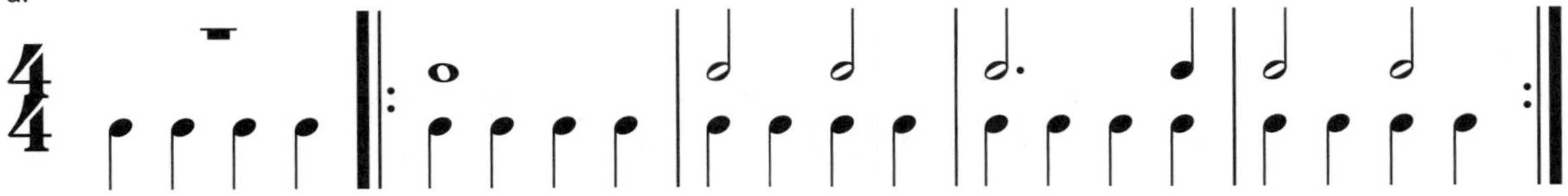

b.

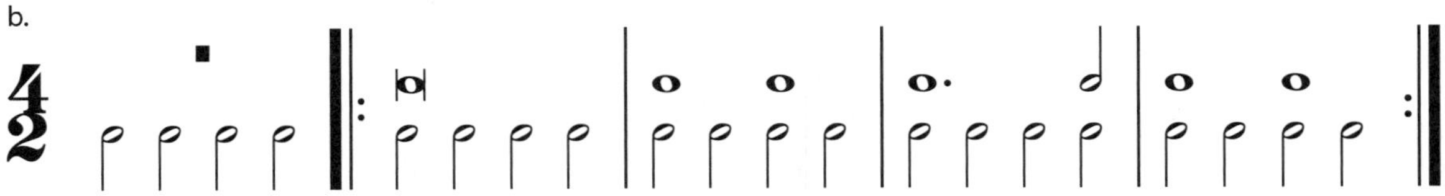

c.

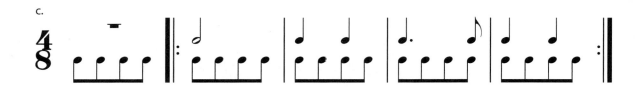

2 Tap *Rhythm 17* with the CD (track 41), first in its original form, then in the other two versions. Study the relationship among the three examples.

a.

b.

c.

3 Write the following rhythms two other ways, as in the exercises above. Double the value of the basic pulse, then halve it.

a.

b.

4

Tap these three versions of *Rhythm 45* (track 69) with the CD.

Triplets with Different Note Values

Triplets can be written with any note value. Unlike notes that normally are divided into two parts, triplets require a bracket and the number 3 to show that the beat is divided into three parts. Compare the following:

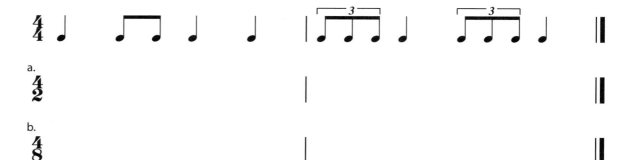

---

5 Write the following rhythm two ways. First double, then halve the value.

a.

b.

---

6 Tap out the rhythm of *Greensleeves* (CD, track 5) along with the recording. Follow the original version (a) for the first verse. Follow the alternative notation (b) for the second verse.

7

Rewrite each of these rhythms in the indicated meter.

e.

f.

8 Tap the following pieces from the *Scorebook*.

Dream Song (*Scorebook* 23)

Christmas Has Come (*Scorebook* 66)

Byrd, *Galiarda* (*Scorebook* 17)

En el portal de Belén (*Scorebook* 51)

9 Sing the following melodies.

10 Choose from the following and sing:

> *Dream Song* (*Scorebook* 23)
>
> *Christmas Has Come* (*Scorebook* 66)
>
> Byrd, *Galiarda* (*Scorebook* 17)
>
> *En el portal de Belén* (*Scorebook* 51)
>
> *Election* (*Scorebook* 68)

TERMS, SYMBOLS, AND CONCEPTS

using different note values for the basic pulse
𝄴 and 𝄵
doubling the value of the basic pulse
dividing the value of the basic pulse

triplets with different note values

Chapter Eleven

Syncopation

We have concentrated thus far on rhythms whose accented notes fall *on* the beat. When accented notes fall *between* beats or *off* the beat, they create **syncopated** rhythms. The fastest way to learn syncopated rhythms is to speak them. In the following exercise, use the speaking system that we learned in Chapter One.

1

Speak *Rhythms 52-54* with the CD (tracks 76–78).

a. *Rhythm 52*: (1 2 3 4)

b. *Rhythm 53*: (1 2 3 4)

c. *Rhythm 54*: (1 2 3 4)

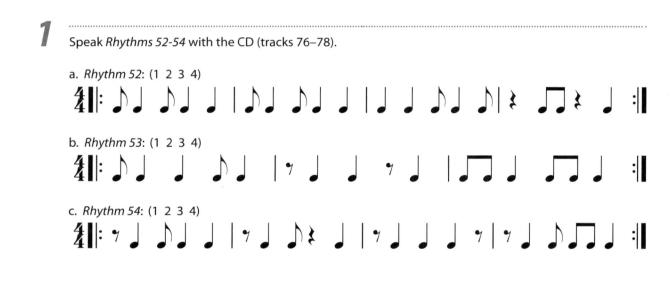

2

Listen to *Rhythms 52a-54a* (CD, tracks 79–81). When you are familiar with the rhythms, tap the upper part.

a. *Rhythm 52a*:

b. *Rhythm 53a*:

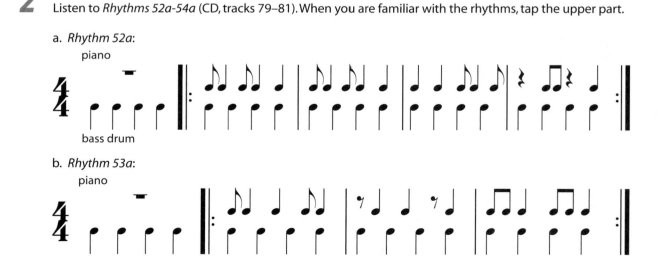

c. *Rhythm 54a*:

Syncopated and Nonsyncopated Rhythms

Notes can occur *on* or *off* the beat. When the note that represents the basic pulse occurs off the beat, the duration of that note extends into the next beat. This phenomenon creates a syncopated rhythmic pattern:

3 ....

Line up the following syncopated rhythms on the Rhythm Spacer.

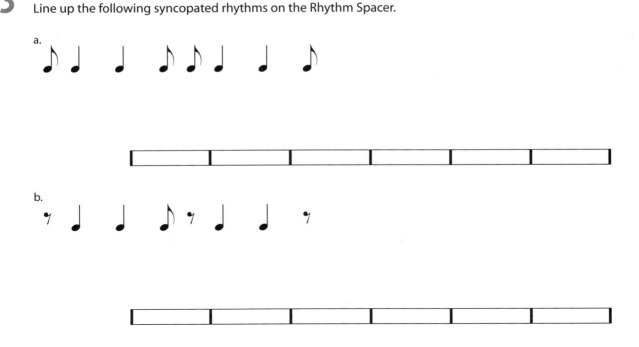

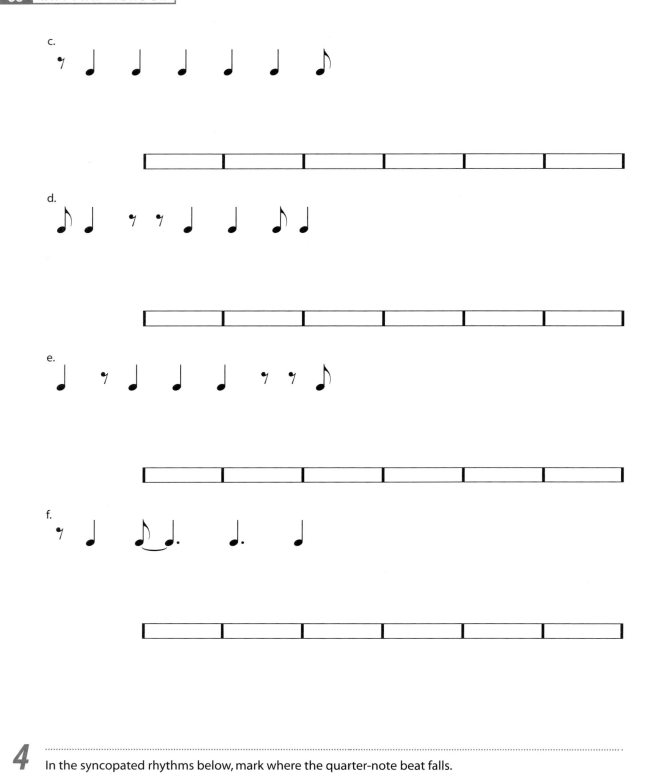

c.

d.

e.

f.

4 In the syncopated rhythms below, mark where the quarter-note beat falls.

a.

b.

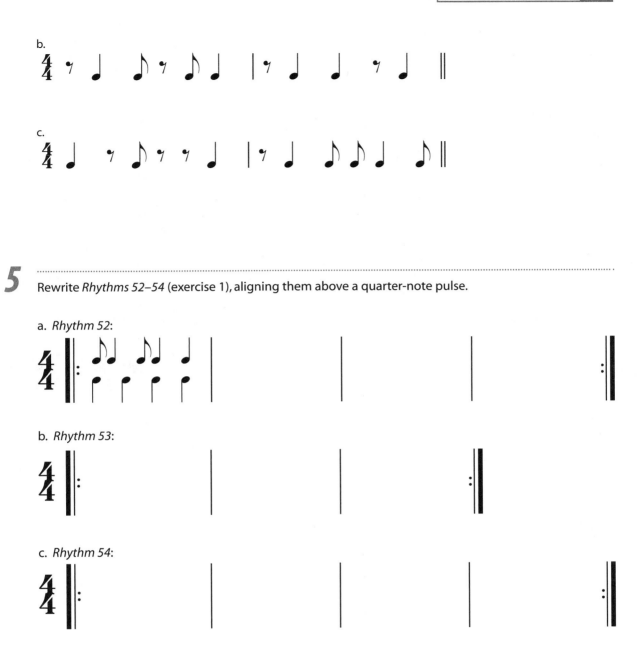

c.

5 Rewrite *Rhythms 52–54* (exercise 1), aligning them above a quarter-note pulse.

a. *Rhythm 52*:

b. *Rhythm 53*:

c. *Rhythm 54*:

6 Rewrite *Rhythm 52* in $\frac{4}{2}$.

7 Rewrite *Rhythm 53* in $\frac{4}{8}$.

8 Listen to *Rhythm 55* (CD, track 82). Notice the syncopation caused by accenting certain sixteenth notes off the beat and changing between different pitched drums.

Rhythm 55:

congas

9 Tap the following pieces from the *Scorebook*.

Carpenter, *Blues for the Rhodes* (*Scorebook* 84)

Latarski, *The Final Blues* (*Scorebook* 85)

10 Sing the following exercises.

a.

11

Choose from the following and sing:

Robin Adair (*Scorebook* 16)

The Hunter (*Scorebook* 24)

Carraig Aonair (*Scorebook* 26)

TERMS, SYMBOLS, AND CONCEPTS

syncopation

counting syncopated and nonsyncopated rhythms

Chapter Twelve

Mixed Meter

Some pieces of music feature changes of meter in quick succession. This type of rhythmic organization is called **mixed meter** and is often found in contemporary classical music, jazz, and music from certain parts of the non-Western world. In the following exercise, the basic pulse of the quarter note remains constant through several metrical changes, even though the number of beats per measure changes.

1

Tap *Rhythms 56–58* along with the CD (tracks 83–85).

a. *Rhythm 56*:

b. *Rhythm 57*:

c. *Rhythm 58*:

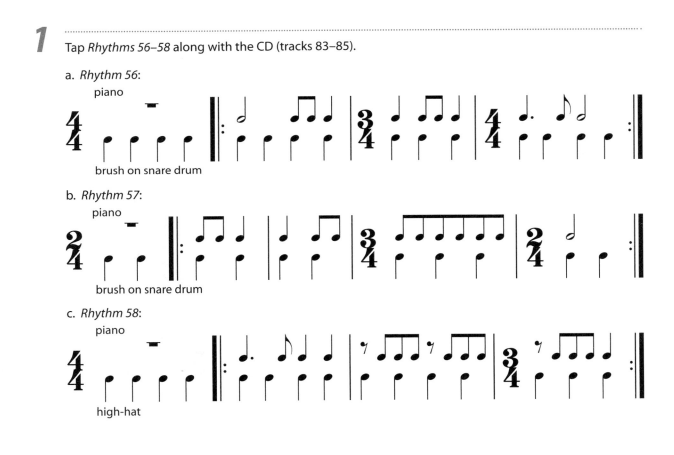

2

Repeat *Rhythms 56–58* without tapping. Count the basic beat with each rhythm, as indicated.

a. *Rhythm 56*:

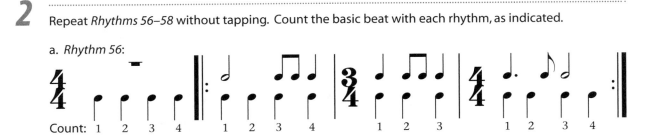

b. *Rhythm 57:*

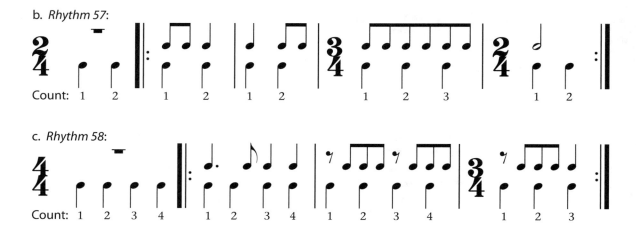

Count: 1   2   1   2   1   2   1   2   3   1   2

c. *Rhythm 58:*

Count: 1   2   3   4   1   2   3   4   1   2   3   4   1   2   3

3 In each of the following exercises, write in the missing meters.

Example

a.

b.

c.

d.

e.

Nonmetered Music

Not all music is written in metered form. In music without meter, there are no bar lines to set off regular metrical groupings. To understand **nonmetered music**, it is important to determine which note serves as the basic pulse, and then to follow that basic pulse throughout the rhythmic pattern. This way, each note receives the appropriate number of beats. In the following examples and in exercise 4, the quarter note serves as the basic pulse.

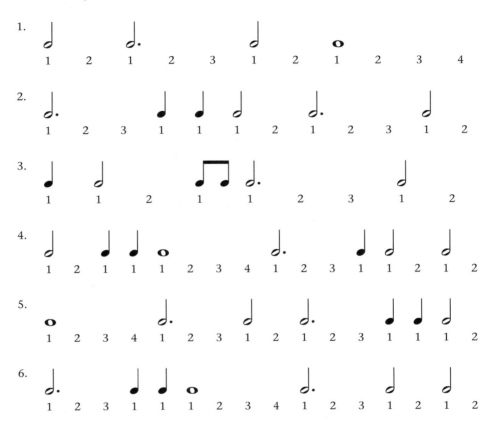

Marking the Basic Pulse

When counting nonmetered music, it is useful to mark where the basic pulse occurs (see p. 48), rather than writing in numbers. Imagining a pulse in this way is actually easier than counting the beats. For example, the rhythms given above can be treated in this way:

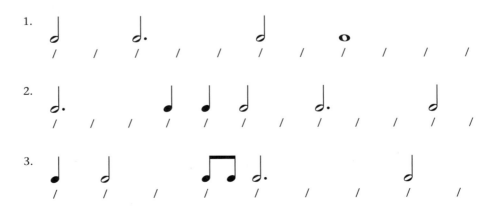

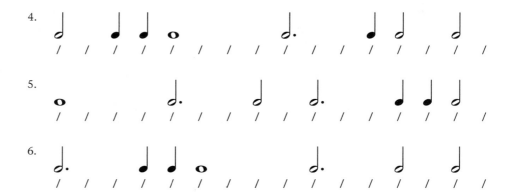

4 Mark the basic pulse below the following rhythms, as in the examples above. Then tap each rhythm, keeping the basic pulse steady.

Complex Meters

Throughout this book, we have focused on meters that feature two, three, or four beats per measure. Certain pieces of music, however, are based in meters that are more complex. These meters usually contain an uneven number of beats per measure; five and seven beats per measure are among the most common. One of the interesting aspects of meters in five or seven is that they divide into unequal groupings within the measure. You may hear a meter of five beats as a grouping of three followed by a grouping of two, or two followed by three. A meter of seven beats may divide into a grouping of three followed by a grouping of four, four followed by three, or two followed by three followed by two. The following examples present only a few of the many possible ways these meters sound.

5   Listen to *Rhythms 59–61* on the CD (tracks 86–88). When you have become familiar with them, tap out the parts.

a. *Rhythm 59*:

b. *Rhythm 60*:

c. *Rhythm 61*:

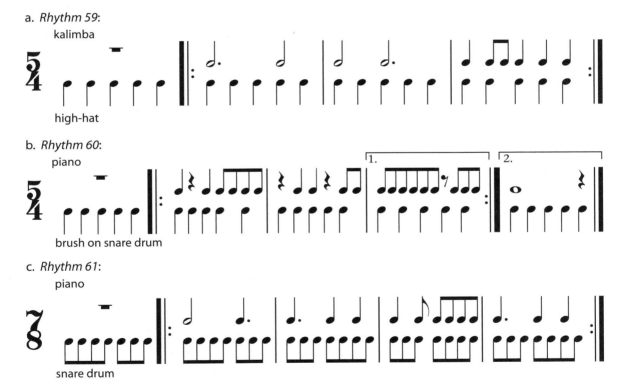

6   Tap the theme from Symphony No. 6 by Tchaikovsky (*Scorebook* 79).

7 Sing the following melodies.

8 Sing the following modal melodies using note names.

　　　　O'er the Burn, Bessie (*Scorebook* 41)

　　　　Andrew Bardon (*Scorebook* 42)

　　　　Peter's Lament (*Scorebook* 43)

TERMS, SYMBOLS, AND CONCEPTS

mixed meter

counting mixed meter

nonmetered music

counting nonmetered music

meter in 5

meter in 7

Table of Note and Rest Values

The value of each of the following symbols is based on the quarter-note unit of one beat.

Name	Symbol	Value (in ♩'s)
whole note	𝅝	4
whole rest	▬	4
half note	𝅗𝅥	2
half rest	▬	2
dotted half note	𝅗𝅥.	3
dotted half rest	▬·	3
quarter note	♩	1
quarter rest	𝄽	1
eighth note	♪	1/2
eighth rest	𝄾	1/2
sixteenth note	𝅘𝅥𝅯	1/4
sixteenth rest	𝄿	1/4
thirty-second note	𝅘𝅥𝅰	1/8
thirty-second rest	𝅀	1/8
sixty-fourth note	𝅘𝅥𝅱	1/16
sixty-fourth rest	𝅁	1/16

Scorebook

Melodies

1 *Come, Let Us Tune*

John Hatton
(d. 1793)

2 Chorale Melody from *Christmas Oratorio*

Johann Sebastian Bach
(1685–1750)

3 *Das walt' Gott Vater und Gott Sohn*

German hymn tune

4 *Fray Diego*   Spanish

5 *Game Song*   Hungarian

6 *Den Vater dort oben*   Sixteenth-century chorale tune

7 *Oliver and the Maiden*   Icelandic

8 *Just As I Am*

William Bradbury
(1816–1868)

9 "Ode to Joy" Theme from Symphony No. 9

Ludwig van Beethoven
(1770–1827)

10 *Brocham Lom*

Gaelic

11 *Lullaby*

Plains Apache

12 *O du schöner Rosengarten*

German

13 *Philis, plus avare que tendre*

French

14 *Music in the Air*

Nineteenth-century American

15 *Repentance*

George Coles
(1792–1858)

16 *Robin Adair*

Traditional

17 Galiarda

William Byrd
(1543–1623)

18 *Die Gedanken sind frei*

German

19 *Drei Reiter um Tor*

German folk song

20 *Lullaby*

Johannes Brahms
(1833–1897)

21 *North River*

William Billings
(1746–1800)

22 *The Trees They Do Grow High*

American

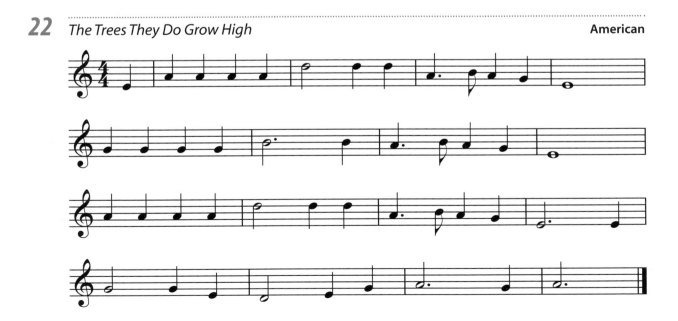

23 *Dream Song*   **Scandinavian**

24 *The Hunter*   **Greek**

25 *In dem Weiten stand ein Haus*   **German**

26 *Carraig Aonair*   **Gaelic**

27 *Que ne suis-je la fougère*   **French**

28 Minuet   **Robert Visée**
                                                                   (c. 1650–c. 1725)

29 *The Knife Sharpener*   **Dutch**

30 *Puer natus in Bethlehem*   **Johann Sebastian Bach**

31 Chorale Melody from *Wedding Cantata*   **Johann Sebastian Bach**

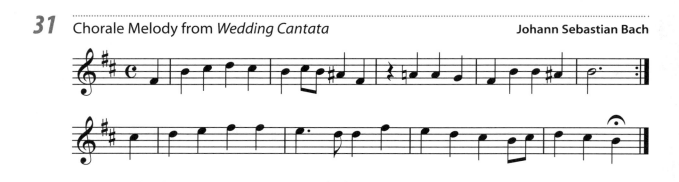

32 Melody   **Finnish**

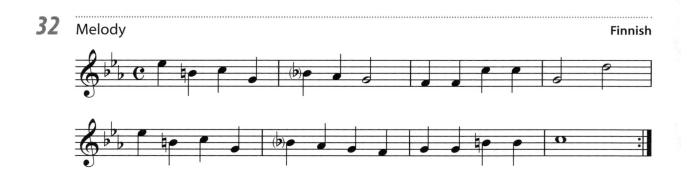

33 *Feinsliebchen*   **German**

34 *Jeune fillette*   **French**

35 *Tyler Street*   **Contemporary American folk tune**

36 Theme from *Sonata Duodecima*, Preludio   **Arcangelo Corelli**
(1653–1713)

37 *Song of the Crow*   **Chinese**

38 *Worksong* **Chinese**

39 *Cherry Blooms* **Japanese**

40 *Cradle Song* **Japanese**

41 *O'er the Burn, Bessie*   **English**

42 *Andrew Bardon*   **American**

43 *Peter's Lament*   **Contemporary American fiddle tune**

44 Hymn   **Armenian**

Melodies with Words

45 *I Know Where I'm Going* **Traditional**

1. I know where I'm go - ing, and I know who's go-ing with me;
I know who I love, but the dear knows who I'll mar - ry.
2. Feath - er beds are soft, and paint - ed rooms are bon - nie; But
I would trade them all for my hand - some, win - some John - nie.

3. I have stockings of silk, and shoes of bright green leather:
   Combs to buckle my hair, and a ring for every finger.

4. Some say he's bad, but I say he's bonnie;
   Fairest of them all is my handsome, winsome Johnnie.

46 *The Water Is Wide* **Traditional**

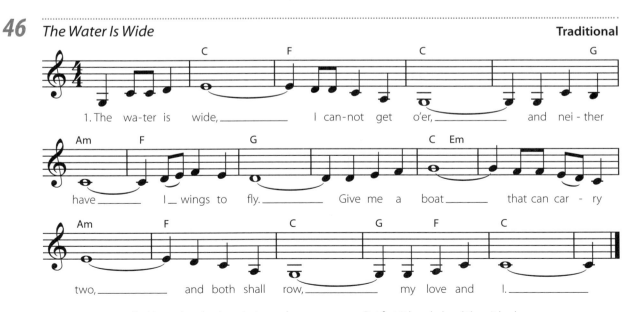

1. The wa-ter is wide,_____ I can-not get o'er,_____ and nei - ther
have_____ I_ wings to fly._____ Give me a boat_____ that can car - ry
two,_____ and both shall row,_____ my love and I._____

2. I leaned my back against an oak,
   Thinking it was a trusty tree;

But first it bended and then it broke,
As thus did my true love to me.

121

47 *Barbrie Allen*

Traditional English

2. All in the merry month of May,
   When green buds they were swelling,
   Young Jonny Grove on his deathbed lay,
   For love of Barbrie Allen.

3. He sent his man unto her then
   To the town where she was dwelling:
   "You must come to my master, dear,
   If your name be Barbrie Allen."
   (this stanza not recorded)

4. So slowly, slowly she came up,
   And slowly she came nigh him,
   And all she said when there she came:
   "Young man, I think you're dying!"

5. He turned his face unto the wall,
   And death was drawing nigh him:
   "Adieu, adieu, my dear friends all,
   Be kind to Barbrie Allen."

48 *Drink to Me Only with Thine Eyes*

Traditional English
Words by Ben Jonson (1616)

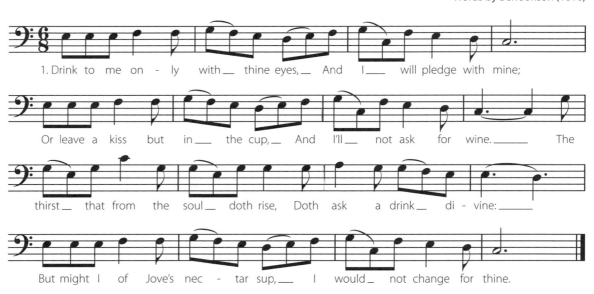

2. I sent thee late a rosy wreath,
   Not so much honoring thee,
   As giving it a hope, that there
   It could not withered be.

   But thou theron did'st only breathe,
   And sent'st it back to me;
   Since when it grows and smells, I swear,
   Not of itself, but thee.

49 *Believe Me If All Those Endearing Young Charms*

Traditional
Words by Thomas Moore (1808)

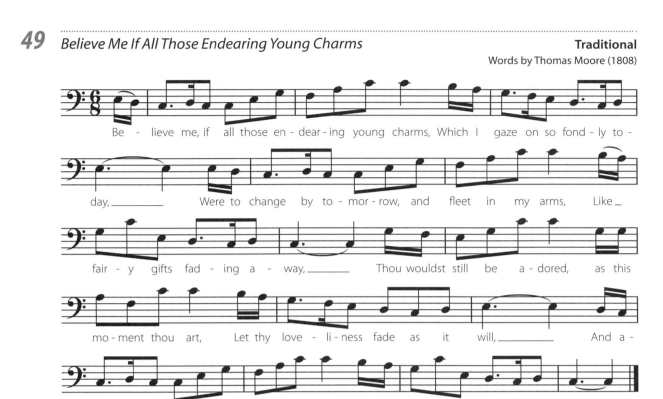

Be - lieve me, if all those en - dear - ing young charms, Which I gaze on so fond - ly to -

day, _____ Were to change by to - mor - row, and fleet in my arms, Like _

fair - y gifts fad - ing a - way, _____ Thou wouldst still be a - dored, as this

mo - ment thou art, Let thy love - li - ness fade as it will, _____ And a -

round the dear ru - in, each wish of my heart, Would en - twine it - self ver - dant - ly still. ____

50 *Amazing Grace*

Traditional

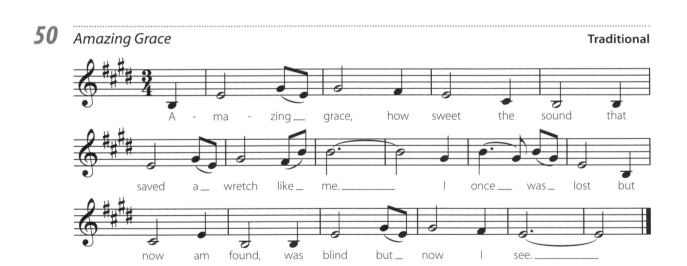

A - ma - zing _ grace, how sweet the sound that

saved a _ wretch like _ me. _____ I once _ was _ lost but

now am found, was blind but _ now I see. _____

51 *En el portal de Belén*   **Spanish Christmas song**

1. En el por - tal _____ de Be - lén. _____ Hay u -
na__ cu - na de vien - to. _____ Es - pa - ra me - cer al
Ni - ño. _____ La no - che__ del _____ Na - ci - mien - to. _____

(At the gates of Bethlehem, there is a cradle of wind. It is to rock the child, the night of the birth.)

2. Los tres Reyes del Oriente
   Guidados por una estrella,
   Fueron a adorar al Niño
   Que nació de una doncella.

2. The three kings of the Orient
   Guided by a star,
   Went to adore the Child
   Who was born of a maiden.

3. De María, Virgen pura,
   Nació Jesús Nazareno,
   Vino por borrar la culpa,
   Que dejó padre primero.

3. Of Mary, pure virgin,
   Was born Jesus of Nazareth,
   Came to erase the sins
   Which were left by the first father.

52 *Dear Willie*   **Traditional**

1. A__ walk - ing and a talk - ing, A walk - ing go__ I, For to
meet my dear Wil - lie I'll meet him by and by. 2. For to
meet him is a plea - sure, but part - ing is__ grief. And a
false heart - ed lov - er is worse than a thief.

3. For a thief he will rob you and take what you have
   But a false hearted lover will lead you to the grave.

4. And the grave will consume you and turn you to dust.
   Not one boy in twenty a poor girl can trust.

(repeat first verse)

53 *La paloma*

Spanish

Es la Pa-lo-ma di-vi-na La que nun-ca tu-vo man-cha, Pa-ra su-bir a su ni-do su dul-ce vue-lo le-van-ta. Ma-rí-a Ma-rí-a lle-na de gra-cia.

(It is the divine dove, the one that never had a stain.
She takes sweet flight to reach her next. Mary, Mary, full of grace.)

54 *The Oak and the Ash*

Traditional English

1. A north coun-try maid up to Lon-don had stayed Al-though with her na-ture

did not a-gree. She wept and she sighed and bit-ter-ly she cried. I

wish once a-gain in the north I could be. Oh, the oak and the ash and the

bon-nie i-vy tree, do flou-rish at home in my own coun-try.

2. Oh, would I be in the North Country,
   Where the lads and the lassies are making the hay;
   I delighted to see what is dearest to me,
   When a mischievous light somehow took me away.
   Oh, the oak and the ash and the bonnie ivy tree,
   Do flourish at home in my own country.

3. At wakes and at fairs, being void of all cares,
   We there with our lovers did play and did dance;
   Then mistakenly I my fortune did try,
   And so to London my steps did advance.
   Oh, the oak and the ash and the bonnie ivy tree,
   Do flourish at home in my own country.

55 *Henry Martin*   **Traditional**

1. There were three broth-ers in mer-ry Scot-land, In Scot-land there lived broth-ers three. And they did cast lots which of them should go, should go, should go, should go, For to turn rob-ber all on the salt sea.

2. The lot it did fall upon Henry Martin,
The youngest of all the three,
That he should go, he should go,
should go, should go, should go,
For to turn robber all on the salt sea.

3. He had not been sailing a long winter's night,
And part of a long winter's day,
Before he espied a lofty stout ship,
stout ship, stout ship,
Come along down on him straight away.

56 *Greensleeves*   **Traditional**

1. A - las my love, you do me wrong to cast me off dis-cour-teous-ly, And I have lov - ed you so long, De - light - ing in your com - pa - ny. Green - sleeves was all my joy, Green - sleeves was my de - light, Green - sleeves was my heart of gold And who but my la - dy Green - sleeves.

2. I have been ready at your hand
to grant whatever you desire;
I have both waged life and land,
your love and goodwill for to have.
Greensleeves (etc.)

3. If you intend thus to disdain,
it does the more enrapture me;
And even so I still remain
a lover in captivity.
Greensleeves (etc.)

4. And yet thou wouldst not love me,
thou couldst desire no earthly thing;
Still thou hadst it readily,
thy music still to play and sing.
Greensleeves (etc.)

Rounds, Canons, and Part Songs

57 *Dona nobis pacem* **Traditional round**

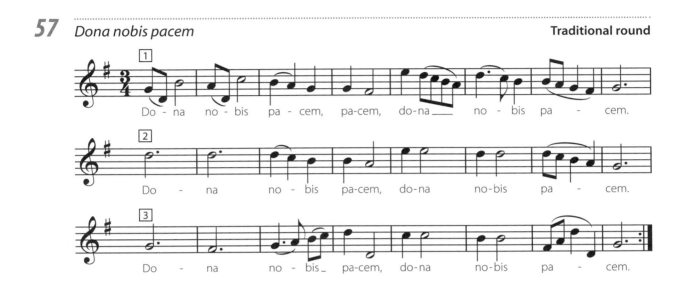

58 *Oh How Lovely Is the Evening* **Traditional German round**

59 *Hey, Ho, Nobody at Home* **Traditional English round**

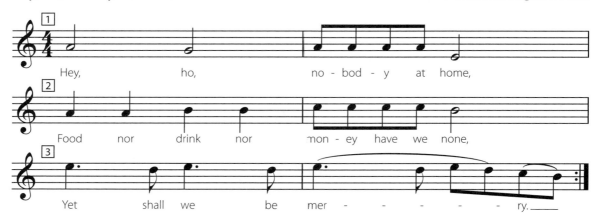

Hey, ho, no-bod-y at home,

Food nor drink nor mon-ey have we none,

Yet shall we be mer - - - - ry.____

60 *The Welcome Song* **Traditional American canon**

Wel-come, wel-come eve-ry guest, wel-come to our mu-sic fest.

Mu-sic is our on-ly __ cheer, fills both soul and __ ra-vished ear.

Sa-cred nine __ teach us the mood, sweet-est notes to __ be ex-plored.

Gen-tly moves the trem-bling __ air to __ com-plete our __ con-cert fair.

61 *Shalom Chaverim* **Traditional Israeli round**

Sha - lom cha-ve-rim, sha - lom cha-ve-rim, sha - lom, sha - lom, Le

hit - ra - ot, le hit - ra - ot, sha - lom, sha - lom.

(Farewell good friends, farewell good friends, farewell, farewell,
'Til we meet again, 'till we meet again, farewell, farewell.)

62 *The Blue Note Canon*

From *Canons Old and New*
(used by permission)

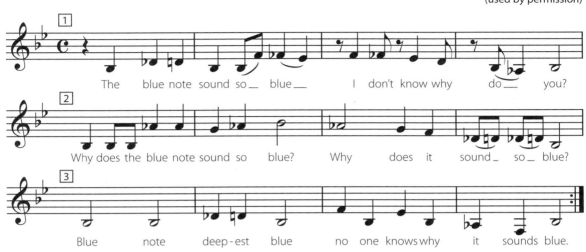

The blue note sound so __ blue __ I don't know why do __ you?

Why does the blue note sound so blue? Why does it sound __ so __ blue?

Blue note deep-est blue no one knows why it sounds blue.

63 *Ringing of the Bells*

From *The Hirsau Book of Carols*
(used by permission)

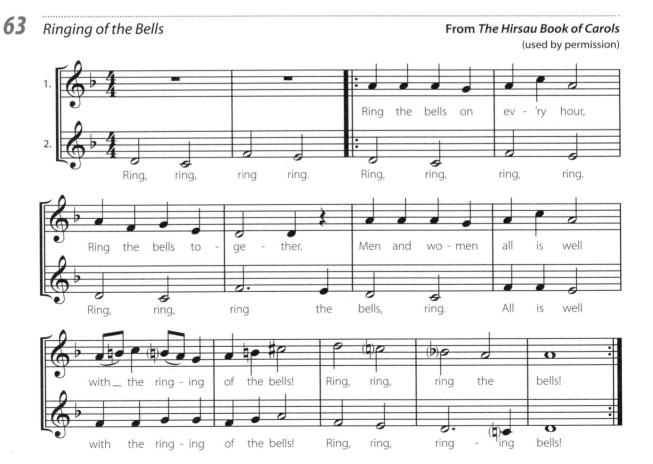

1.

2.

Ring, ring, ring ring. Ring, ring, ring, ring.

Ring the bells on ev - 'ry hour,

Ring the bells to - ge - ther. Men and wo - men all is well

Ring, ring, ring the bells, ring. All is well

with __ the ring - ing of the bells! Ring, ring, ring the bells!

with the ring - ing of the bells! Ring, ring, ring - ing bells!

64 *Planting Song*

From *The Hirsau Book of Carols*
(used by permission)

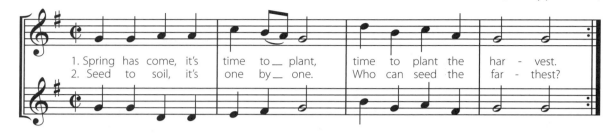

1. Spring has come, it's time to _ plant, time to plant the har - vest.
2. Seed to soil, it's one by _ one. Who can seed the far - thest?

Win - ter now is _ gone, And the win - ter's cold - ness.

Now the days grow _ long, the sun shines now with bold - ness.

65 *Willie, Take Your Little Drum*

Burgundian carol

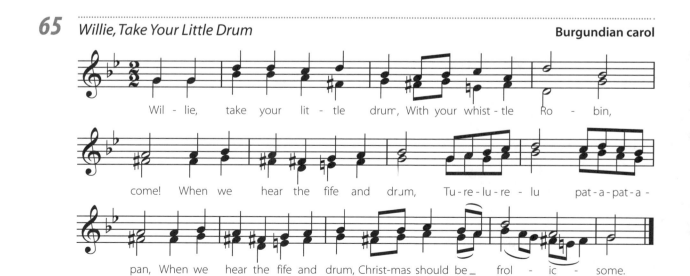

Wil - lie, take your lit - tle drum, With your whist - tle Ro - bin, come! When we hear the fife and drum, Tu - re - lu - re - lu pat - a - pat - a - pan, When we hear the fife and drum, Christ-mas should be _ frol - ic - some.

66 *Christmas Has Come*

From *The Hirsau Book of Carols*
(used by permission)

1. Christ - mas has come and the snow's on the hill, ____
2. Door - ways now o - pen ___ for ev' - ry guest, ____

Turn - ing no long - er, the si - lent ___ mill; Al - le - lu - ia
All gen - tle peo - ple are now at ___ rest;

be of good cheer, ___ Al - le - lu - ia Christ - mas is ___ here!

67 *All the Stars*

From *The Hirsau Book of Carols*
(used by permission)

1. All the stars, turn with time, like an end - less rhym - ing.

All the earth, all the sky, up to heav - en climb - ing.

2. Day and night, night and day, dance with one another.
   Time and task, faith will last, once it is discovered.

3. Dark and light, all is right, when the stars are singing;
   Harmonies, always please; music, love is bringing.

(repeat first verse)

68 *Silent Night*

Melody by Franz Gruber
(1787–1863)
Words by Joseph Mohr

Si – lent night, ho – ly night. All is calm, all is bright.

'Round yon vir – gin, moth – er and child, ho – ly in – fant so ten – der and mild,

Sleep in heav – en – ly peace,____ sleep__ in heav – en – ly peace.

Chorales

69 *Election*

William Billings
(1746–1800)

1. Thou art my blest Por - tion, thou _ dear Na - za - rene. Who
1. Thou art my blest Por - tion, thou dear Na - za - rene. Who _
1. Thou art my blest Por - tion, thou dear Na - za - rene. Who _
1. Thou art my blest Por - tion, thou dear Na - za - rene. Who

once was op - press-ed. _ And _ sore - ly dis - tress-ed. When thou didst lie _ un - der my
once was op - press-ed. And sore - ly dis - tress-ed. When thou didst lie un - der my
once was op - press-ed. And sore - ly dis - tress-ed. When thou didst lie un - der my
once was op - press-ed. And sore - ly dis - tress-ed. When thou didst lie un - der my

Curse and my Shame, To save me for ev - er, a - dor'd be thy Name.
Curse and my Shame, To save me for ev - er, a - dor'd be thy Name.
Curse and my Shame, To save me for ev - er, a - dor'd be thy Name.
Curse and my Shame, To _ save me for ev - er, a - dor'd be thy Name.

2. There in that deep Wound, I view in thy Side,
   I see my Election, And all my Perfection;
   Beholding the Glory of thy Blood-bought Bride,
   Amongst the dear Number who in thee confide.

3. Now I can behold thee, Love, bleeding for me!
   I bow to none other But thee, my dear Lover.
   With Wonder I view thee on the bloody Tree,
   And hear thee, Lamb, crying, 'Tis finish'd for thee:

4. That Moment I prov'd the Grace of thy Name,
   Where all Things I wanted Unto me was granted;
   Yea, mine is thy Fullness that's always the same,
   That still I might praise thee thou meek slaughter'd Lamb.

70 *Komm, Gott Schöpfer*

Johann Sebastian Bach

Komm, Gott Schö - pfer, hei - li - ger Geist,
be - such das Herz der Men - schen dein,
mit Gna - den sie füll, wie du weisst,
dass dein Ge - schöpf vor - hin sein.

71 **Chorale from Cantata No. 43**   **Johann Sebastian Bach**

1. Du Le - bens fürst,_____ Herr Je - su Christ, der du bist auf -
gen Him - mel, da_____ dein Va - ter ist und die Ge - mein'

ge - nom - - men wie soll ich dei - nen gro - ssen Sieg,
der From - - men:

den du durch ei - - - nen schwe - ren Krieg er - wor - hen

hast, recht prei - sen, und dir g'nug Ehr' er - wei - sen?

2. Zieh' uns dir nach, so laufen wir,
gib uns des Glaubens Flügel;
hilf, dass wir fliehen weit von hier
auf Israelis Hügel!
Mein Gott, wann fahr' ich doch dahin,
wo ich ohn' Ende fröhlich bin?
wann werd' ich vor dir stehen,
dein Angesicht zu sehen?

72 *Psalm 75*

Heinrich Schütz
(c. 1585–1672)

Aus un - sers Her - zens Grun - de dan - ken wir Gott, dem Herrn,
ver - künd - gen Sei - ne Wun - der, sa - gen sein Na - men Ehr,

dass er uns ist so na - he mit sei - nem Se - gen

mild, Schafft, das wir Trost emp - fan - gen, wenn er aus

Nö - ten hilft, _____ wenn er aus Nö - ten hilft. _____

73 Prologue from *Prophetiae sibyllarum*

Orlando di Lasso
(1530/32–1594)

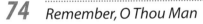

74 *Remember, O Thou Man*

Thomas Ravenscroft
(c. 1582–c. 1635)

A Christmas carol

2. Remember God's goodnesse,
   O thou man, O thou man,
   Remember God's goodnesse
   And his promise made.
   Remember God's goodnesse,
   How he sent his son doubtlesse
   Our sinnes for to redresse, be not affraid.

3. The Angels all did sing,
   O thou man, O thou man,
   The Angels all did sing
   Upon Shepheards hill.
   The Angels all did sing
   Praises to our heavenly King.
   And peace to man living with a good will.

From the Classical Tradition

75 *Nancie*

Thomas Morley
(1557/58–1602)

76 Theme from *Don Giovanni*

Wolfgang Amadeus Mozart

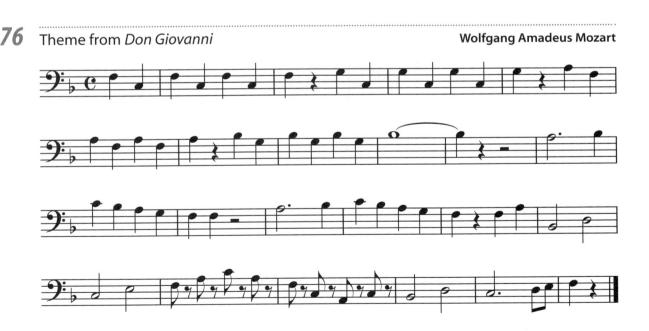

77 Sarabanda from Concerto Grosso, Op. 6, No. 11 — Arcangelo Corelli

78 Theme from Piano Sonata No. 19 — Ludwig van Beethoven

79 Theme from Symphony No. 6 — Pyotr Il'yich Tchaikovsky
(1840–1893)

80 Minuet

Wolfgang Amadeus Mozart

81 Prelude

Frédéric Chopin
(1810–1849)

*See Supplementary Guide III for the harmony of this chord.

82 Sonata in E Major

Domenico Scarlatti
(1685–1757)

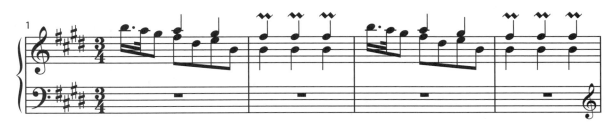

* Repeats not played on CD.

83 *Blues for the Rhodes*

Tom Carpenter

© 2000

84 *Pocket Full of Blues*

Don Latarski

© 2000

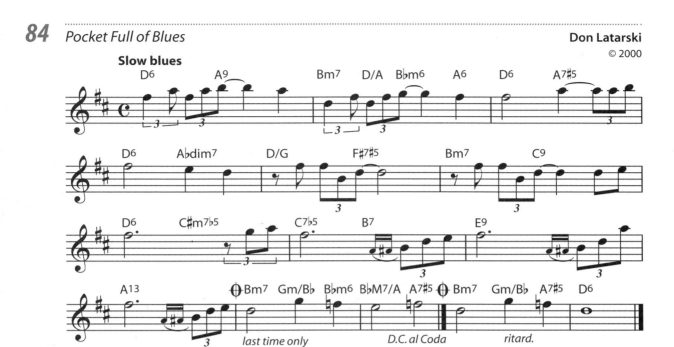

85 *The Final Blues*

Don Latarski

© 1994